marshmallows

100 MOUTHWATERING MARSHMALLOW TREATS

TIM KINNAIRD

marshmallows

100 MOUTHWATERING MARSHMALLOW TREATS

BARRON'S

A QUINTET BOOK

First edition for the United States
and Canada published in 2014 by
Barron's Educational Series, Inc.

All inquiries should be addressed to:
Barron's Educational Series, Inc.
250 Wireless Boulevard
Hauppauge, NY 11788
www.barronseduc.com

Library of Congress Control Number: 2013957096
ISBN: 978-1-4380-0423-5
QTT.MMLL

Conceived, designed, and produced by:
Quintet Publishing
4th Floor, Sheridan House
114-116 Western Road
Hove BN3 1DD
UK

Project Editor: Julie Brooke
Designer: Lucy Parissi
Photographer: Jon Whitaker
Food Stylist: Uyen Luu
Art Director: Michael Charles
Managing Editor: Emma Bastow
Publisher: Mark Searle

Manufactured in China by 1010 Printing International Ltd.

9 8 7 6 5 4 3 2 1

CONTENTS

INTRODUCTION

Food has the ability to do many things. It can excite, soothe, tease, or comfort. Some food is serious, other food is light and passing. Marshmallows … well marshmallows are the mischievous children, staying up late laughing, smiling, and telling jokes until you can't help but join in their bouncy party.

The recipes and advice in this book are intended to be relaxed, easy, and—more than anything else—fun. Happily, most people don't know how easy marshmallows are to make. The basic recipe is something that, with practice, can be made in 10 minutes with only four ingredients. Hooray for that. Wowing your co-workers with some—they were just something I made at home—triple layered marshmallows, couldn't be easier. Walk tall at the school bake sale as your homemade salt caramel marshmallows sell out first. Throw out those self-help books—marshmallows are the key to social success and personal contentment. Honestly.

Marshmallows originate from the mallow plant. *Althaea officinalis* is native to Europe and Africa, and when crushed, releases a thick, gloopy mucilage. In ancient Greece it was recommended to relieve wounds, swellings, and all sorts of inflamed body parts. Apparently, it was particularly efficacious once boiled in wine. The ancient Egyptians first used it as a food and to set a confectionery made from egg white and sugar. As with much of today's candies, the French refined the marshmallow in the nineteenth century and started using gelatin in place of the plant extract.

Most commercially available marshmallows are far removed from those early original treats. What's widely available now has its place, but is dense and dull compared with what you will quickly master at home. Using egg white as the basis of marshmallows is the key difference and gives them a light and delicate texture.

We make and sell lots of marshmallows in our store. On quieter days, or if we're feeling virtuous, we give out free marshmallows to try. The response is always the same: "oh, that's lovely—it's so light." More than anything else we might try, it surprises.

Then there's what happens to marshmallows when you heat them up. Melting marshmallows under a flame transforms them from fun candies into a complex mix of burned sugar and molten vanilla. With marshmallows, still waters run deep. From the simple s'more to marshmallow-infused cocktails, melt them and they turn edgy.

Making marshmallows is an excellent way to experiment and get creative in the kitchen. While a light and fluffy vanilla marshmallow is perfect in itself, it is also a springboard for a journey into a sweet and bouncy universe. Let marshmallows be your confectionery canvas. Marshmallows are easily flavored and do a remarkable job of losing their intrinsic mallowyness and absorbing the flavors around them. That's what the recipes in this book aim to achieve.

As important as clear and bright flavors are, marshmallows work because of their texture. Their bounciness requires chewing, and that heightens the flavor. Contrasting that with crunchy, creamy, or even fizzy coatings adds immeasurably to the eating fun. It increases the surprise and excitement.

Shaping and molding marshmallows is easy. Modern silicone molds and baking pans offer an infinite world of shaping. From geometric shapes, yule logs, twists, and lollipops, master the basic recipe and there are hours of fun to be had. Another side to marshmallows is their property as a readymade recipe component. Think of them as pre-prepared meringue. For adding both texture and flavors to mousses, frostings, and toppings, they are a brilliant store cupboard emergency item.

However, more important than anything else, marshmallows and their recipes should be light-hearted and relaxed. Channel your inner eight-year-old, make a mess, and get sticky!

INGREDIENTS

The simplicity of marshmallow making means you can source the core recipe ingredients easily.

Some ingredients work particularly well in marshmallow making. Really good natural fruit extracts and oils should be your best friend and will make the job of flavoring much easier. A few drops added at the last second will transform a mix before setting. Good quality chocolate and unsweetened cocoa will make or break any chocolate creation. A basic marshmallow is a blank canvas for flavor and the chocolate used will shine through.

SUGAR

Sucrose and glucose

Sugar… is sugar, right? Wrong. For successful marshmallow making you'll need sugar in the forms of sucrose and glucose.

Sucrose in the form of superfine sugar is the majority of the sugar used in these recipes. Don't be constrained by plain white superfine sugar though.

Try unrefined variations and even brown sugar to make your marshmallows. They will add complex caramel and vanilla tones and work as a flavoring in themselves. See the brown sugar marshmallow recipe on page 56.

Glucose adds nothing to the taste of marshmallows, but it is used to stop the sucrose from crystallizing. This is particularly important if the marshmallows are to be stored for a while. Purchase from large craft stores or online.

Gelatin

Gelatin can be hard work as the strength and preparations vary. All the recipes here are written for platinum strength leaves. Bloomed sheet gelatin is the easiest preparation to incorporate into a whisking marshmallow mix. As a rule, one leaf will set ⅓ cup (80ml) of liquid. Most recipes in this book require 5 sheets (8g) of platinum strength gelatin.

Gelatin is also available as a powder, but converting between the two is complicated because strengths vary, so I recommend using leaves. However, if you want to use powder, look at the package to see how many cups of liquid it will set, then work out how many packages you will need and follow the package instructions.

Some of the recipes in this book will give softer set marshmallows than others. Chocolate and higher fat ingredients will thicken the mix. Fruit purées and any additional liquid will give a lighter but wetter result. The final texture also relates to the amount of gelatin used. Feel free to add another sheet or take one away according to your taste.

Eggs

Use eggs that are a few days old. As eggs are stored, the egg white component becomes more liquefied. This form of egg white whisks up a little more readily and will give your marshmallows an even lighter texture. The same effect can be achieved if you separate your egg whites in advance and store them in a covered bowl overnight in a refrigerator.

Colorings

Make use of the natural food colorings that are available. The color will heighten the taste. Colorings can also be used to decorate. Once a marshmallow is poured into a baking pan to set, swirl dots through it to give an appetizing ripple.

Handling and measuring glucose syrup can be the definition of sticky. Wet your hands and any tools used to measure it out, such as spoons, spatulas, etc. A good tip to stop the glucose syrup from sticking to the bowl when transferring it to a saucepan for heating, is to spoon the glucose out onto the weighed-out sugar. The sugar will coat the sticky syrup and make it easy to tip out.

EQUIPMENT

Free-standing mixers

There's a road that most home bakers and confectionery makers travel down—the road to a free-standing mixer.

At first, you use whisks and wooden spoons. An easy step up is the handheld electric whisk. At the end of that road is the free-standing mixer. Maybe you'll be inspired by a new job, birthday, or divorce, but one day you'll have an epiphany and buy one— and you will wonder how you ever got by without it. They make marshmallow making easy. Yes, it is doable without, but it is harder work. Go on ... you deserve it.

Thermometers

You'll need something accurate and digital, and no, that old meat thermometer that tells you your holiday turkey is done isn't going to cut it. Choose wisely. An instant-read digital candy thermometer is preferable as the temperature of the sugar syrup rises quite quickly toward the magic 250°F (120°C) and your thermometer needs to keep up. A thermometer that clips to the side of the saucepan and holds the tip nicely in the middle of the syrup frees up your hands. You need to ensure that the thermometer isn't touching the bottom of the saucepan or else you'll get an inaccurately high reading.

Bowl scrapers and spatulas

A bowl scraper and offset spatula are invaluable tools in handling and shaping the warm marshmallow mix. Running the spatula under warm water before smoothing the marshmallow helps flatten and shape it more easily.

Pastry bags and molds

Shaping marshmallows is half the fun of making them. Fill a pastry bag with marshmallow mix and you can easily pipe mini marshmallows to tumble into hot chocolate or long strips that can be twisted into shapes. Silicone molds are great for creating perfectly smooth and even shapes. Lightly oil the molds and fill with marshmallow mix for a sharp finish.

Storing

Marshmallows benefit from a period of time at room temperature and exposure to the air before storing. This helps them develop a slight crust as they mature and dry out. That gives a great textural contrast. After that, store them in an airtight container and eat within a week to ten days.

Food allergies

Happily, none of the ingredients in a basic marshmallow recipe contain gluten. It's also easy enough to choose variations of that recipe that use gluten-free flavorings and coatings. Also included in this book are recipes for egg-free and vegan marshmallows.

THE VANILLA MARSHMALLOW MOTHERSHIP

The start of your marshmallow journey begins here. This is the core recipe on which many of the variations that follow in the book are based. There's a bit of technique and judgment required in perfecting the lightest and most delicious marshmallows, but not that much.

Using egg white in the recipe gives a much lighter marshmallow. (See pages 12 and 13 for egg-free and vegan recipes.) Basically, this recipe is a meringue made with hot sugar syrup that is combined with gelatin. That's as easy as it sounds.

Making marshmallows can be messy. In many ways that's half the fun of making them. Unless you want to find crusted-on bits of sugary goodness behind your ears two days later at work, prepare and plan. If you're not bothered, dive straight in and immerse yourself in sticky sweetness. Mmm.

INGREDIENTS
For about 30 (1-inch/2.5cm) marshmallow cubes

Plain marshmallow:
5 sheets (¼ ounce/8g) platinum-strength leaf gelatin
1 teaspoon vegetable oil
1 egg white (1 ¼ ounces/35g)
1 ¼ cups (280g) superfine sugar
1 ½ tablespoons (25ml) glucose syrup
1 teaspoon vanilla extract (or other flavoring)

50/50 coating:
½ cup (50g) confectioners' sugar
½ cup (50g) cornstarch

METHOD

1. Place the gelatin sheets in a bowl of cold water and let them soften or "bloom." This should take about 10 minutes. Make sure the water is cold. If it's warm, the gelatin will start to melt.

2. Lightly grease an 8-inch (20cm) square baking pan with the oil.

3. Place the egg white in the bowl of a free-standing mixer. A handheld electric mixer can also be used. Mix together the superfine sugar, glucose syrup,

and 4 tablespoons (60ml) water in a small saucepan until the mixture feels like wet sand. Place a digital candy thermometer in the saucepan and bring to a boil over medium heat. There is no need to stir the mixture. As you heat the sugar syrup, sugar crystals may form on the side of the saucepan. A heatproof pastry brush dipped in cold water can be used to dissolve and disperse this sugar. When the syrup reaches 240°F (115°C), start to whisk the egg white until it forms stiff peaks.

4. After 4–5 minutes the sugar syrup will hit 250°F (120°C). Pour it slowly and carefully down the side of the bowl while whisking the egg whites at medium speed. Avoid pouring the hot sugar syrup onto the beaters as they will spray hot sugar around the kitchen and cause lumps in the mix.

5. While the meringue mix is whisking, squeeze the excess water from the gelatin sheets. After 2–3 minutes, add the softened gelatin sheets directly into the mix, still continuing to whisk.

6. Add the vanilla or other flavoring.

7. Continue to whisk for an additional 3–4 minutes until the mixture is thick and stiff. The mix needs to hold its shape but still be workable. You can't overwhisk at this stage, but if it cools too much, the marshmallow will be very difficult to shape or mold. You'll never get it out of the bowl!

8. Scrape the warm mix out into the oiled baking pan and smooth evenly with an offset spatula.

9. Mix the confectioners' sugar and cornstarch in a small bowl. Dust the top of the marshmallow with a fine layer of the mixture and let set for 4–6 hours or preferably overnight. Cut the marshmallow into chunks and drop them into the sugar and cornstarch mixture to coat them. Store in an airtight container for up to 1 week.

TIPS

Most marshmallow recipes recommend dusting the bottom of the baking pan with cornstarch and confectioners' sugar before you pour in the marshmallow mixture. I think this makes it harder to spread the marshmallow evenly. When dusted, the warm marshmallow mix has a tendency to move around as one lump, and pockets of confectioners' sugar and cornstarch can form underneath. Oiling the pan allows the marshmallow to be removed easily and produces a smooth, flat bottom.

50/50 MARSHMALLOW COATING

The 50/50 confectioners' sugar and cornstarch coating used here is used throughout this book and should be your go-to coating. It can be livened up easily with colorings and flavorings such as fruit powders, finely chopped nuts, and edible lusters.

FREE-FROM VARIATIONS

Marshmallows can be made easily without egg. The gelatin alone gives the marshmallow its structure. It's worth trying this recipe, as it gives a slightly denser marshmallow and it's even simpler than the egg white-based version.

EGG-FREE

INGREDIENTS

1 teaspoon vegetable oil
5 sheets (¼ ounce/8g) platinum-strength leaf gelatin
1 ¼ cups (280g) superfine sugar
1 ½ tablespoons (25ml) glucose syrup
1 teaspoon vanilla extract (or other flavoring)
1 quantity 50/50 coating (see page 10)

METHOD

Lightly grease a baking pan with the oil.

Soak the gelatin sheets in a bowl of cold water until soft. Squeeze out the excess water from the gelatin sheets and place in a small saucepan with 2 tablespoons water.

Meanwhile, heat the superfine sugar, glucose syrup, and 4 tablespoons (60ml) water in a small saucepan over moderate heat until it registers 250°F (120°C) on a digital candy thermometer.

While the sugar syrup is heating, warm the gelatin over very low heat until it melts. Pour the molten gelatin into the bowl of a free-standing mixer and whisk for 2 minutes.

Pour the hot sugar syrup down the side of the bowl onto the gelatin while still whisking. Be careful to avoid the actual beaters, or you'll cover the kitchen with hot sugar. Whisk until the mixture is stiff and thick but still workable. Add the vanilla or other flavoring and tip out into the oiled baking pan.

Dust the top of the marshmallow with a fine layer of 50/50 coating mix and let set for 4–6 hours or preferably overnight. Cut the marshmallow into chunks and coat them in the 50/50 coating mix. Store in an airtight container for up to 1 week.

Makes 20 (1 ¼-inch/3cm) marshmallow cubes

TIP

All the recipes in this book will work well using this variation. You'll achieve a slightly different result texture-wise, but it will still be delicious and lovely.

VEGAN

This recipe is fascinating. It's worth trying even if you're not following a vegan diet. The egg white is replaced by a soy protein and the gelatin by a seaweed extract called carrageenan. It's based on the open source recipe from Dave Soleil's blog: www.veganmarshmallows.blogspot.co.uk.

INGREDIENTS
1 teaspoon vegetable oil
5 tablespoons soy protein isolate
  (see notes below)
2 teaspoons baking powder
¼ teaspoon guar gum
1 ½ cups (300g) superfine sugar
  (see notes below)
1 ½ tablespoons (25ml) glucose syrup
1 tablespoon carrageenan (see notes below)
1 teaspoon flavoring
1 quantity 50/50 coating
  (see page 10)

NOTES
The soy protein isolate can be found in health stores and the pharmacy section of some supermarkets. Otherwise, it can be obtained online.

Carrageenan is sold as vegegel or vegetarian gelatin in supermarkets. Check the ingredients on the package. It can also be bought online.

Check the vegan credentials of your superfine sugar with the manufacturer's website.

METHOD
Lightly grease a baking pan with the oil.

Mix together the soy protein, baking powder, guar gum, and ¾ cup (180ml) water in the bowl of a free-standing mixer. Whisk for 8–10 minutes. The initial pale brown paste will be transformed into a lighter white cream, and stiff peaks will form.

Next is the tricky part. Place the superfine sugar, glucose syrup, and ½ cup (125ml) water in a large saucepan and stir to combine. Warm slightly over medium heat until you have a smooth syrup. Sprinkle in the carrageenan and whisk it in to incorporate. Stir continuously, using a digital candy thermometer to measure the temperature. The carrageenan will naturally cause the sugar mixture to set around the sides of the saucepan. Use a stiff spatula or spoon to keep the sides as clear as possible. Otherwise, the stuck sugar will begin to caramelize, discoloring the mix and creating lumps. Continue to heat to 230°F (110°C). By this stage, the mixture will be thick and extraordinarily sticky. Swiftly tip the syrup onto the soy protein mix while still whisking. Don't scrape in any sugar that has stuck to the sides of the saucepan as it will cause lumps.

Continue to whisk until stiff and thick, then add flavoring, tip out into the oiled baking pan, and let set.

When the marshmallow is set, cut and dust with the 50/50 coating mix.

Makes 30 large marshmallows

FLAVORING, COATING & SHAPING

Tempting as it is to use the phrase "let your imagination run wild" to convey the sense that flavoring, coating, and shaping your marshmallows should be seen an opportunity to go bananas in the kitchen, I'll resist the temptation, but . . .

In the following recipes there are lots of flavor combinations. Many of those are tried and tested classics, some a little unusual. Any sweet flavor combinations you might come across in cakes, confectionery, chocolate, or ice creams will almost certainly work well in a marshmallow.

Incorporating flavors can be a little tricky, as some ingredients will cause the marshmallow mix to collapse and fail. Those ingredients high in fat are particularly difficult. Chocolate causes problems because the cocoa butter will flatten your whisking mix within seconds. The best method is to fold the chocolate in at the last minute or coat the marshmallow in chocolate.

FLAVOR DROPS, OILS & EXTRACTS

An extraordinary range of flavor compounds and drops is available. In supermarkets, vanilla, lemon, coffee, rose, and orange water are easy enough to find. Look beyond the baking ingredients section for other inspiration. Dried whole and ground spices such as cardamom, saffron, cinnamon, and even pepper make good choices. Finely grind them as part of a coating or infuse into the sugar syrup to flavor the marshmallow itself.

Specialist confectionery and chocolate suppliers stock a wide array of flavorings in the form of extracts and essences. From mandarin to orchids, and blue cheese to apple pie, the choice is vast. Natural extracts tend to make better marshmallows and are much more wholesome. See Resources, page 144, for information on where to get hold of them.

FRUIT POWDERS

Freeze-dried fruits in the form of whole fruit and powders are fabulous at packing flavor into a marshmallow. Both can be used as an ingredient in the marshmallow itself, but perhaps it is even better to use a fruit powder as part of the coating.

USING CORDIALS & SYRUPS

Off the shelf fruit cordials are a readymade marshmallow ingredient. Pour in 3–4 tablespoons during the final marshmallow whisking for both flavor and color. Look out for the more unusual flavors as well as soda syrups—root beer marshmallow anyone?

OTHER COATINGS

If you can coat a chocolate, cake, cookie, or candy in it you can almost certainly coat a marshmallow in it. Chopped nuts and chocolate flakes are great. Ice-cream toppings such as sprinkles work wonderfully. Think about textural contrast.

MOLDING MARSHMALLOWS

Silicone molds are your friends here. There's a universe of sizes and shapes available. Getting marshmallows out of molds can be difficult, so go for the less intricate. Geometric shapes work best—your favorite magic unicorn mold is going to be much more tricky.

CUTTING MARSHMALLOWS

For me, marshmallows should be precise and even. In our store we use a confectionery guitar cutter, which cuts perfect straight marshmallows every time. Unless you're planning on setting up your own marshmallow business, they are a bit expensive. Use a long, sharp knife and try and cut the marshmallows straight down. It's easy to cut them on a slope. Make lots of marshmallows and practice. An oiled pizza cutting wheel can work well to get an even cut, as can a cheese board and wire.

PIPING MARSHMALLOWS

A pastry bag filled with warm marshmallow is one of the best things to hold. What you do with that bag is almost irrelevant. Think of your piped beauties as confectionery hand warmers, and hold them close. If you must make marshmallow with it ...

Try using fluted tips for small stars, or plain tips for domes and mounds. Whatever shape you choose, work quickly. Marshmallow sets fast and it's easy to get distracted and clog up your tip. A pastry bag is also a great help for filling shapes and molds.

Chapter 1

CLASSICS

Soft, sugary, and so very moreish, these classic marshmallow flavors have
been pleasing our palates for generations. Whether you enjoy traditional
vanilla or Middle Eastern orange and pistachio, these sweet treats will
delight you and your family for decades to come.

BLACKENED VANILLA SUPER MARSHMALLOWS

So there's vanilla, and then there's real vanilla. Think of vanilla like you would wine—different climates give different flavors. This is your chance to track down some heady, sticky, and plump vanilla beans and drift away on a marshmallowy cloud.

INGREDIENTS
4 vanilla beans
1 quantity 50/50 coating (see page 10)
1 quantity ingredients for vanilla marshmallow mix (see page 10)

METHOD
Preheat the oven to 400°F (200°C). Place 2 of the vanilla beans in the oven and bake for 20–25 minutes or until crisp and brittle. Let cool, then grind to dust in a spice grinder.

Mix the vanilla dust with the 50/50 coating in a medium bowl.

Split the remaining vanilla beans and scrape out the seeds.

Make the marshmallow mix following the method on page 10, adding the seeds to the mix at Step 6.

Let marshmallow set, then cut and dust with the vanilla, sugar, and cornstarch mix.

Makes 30 marshmallows

TOP TIPS
As well as Madagascan, try vanilla from Tahiti, India, Mexico, or Uganda (see Resources, page 144). Check out those floral, fruity, and chocolaty aromas.

RICH CHOCOLATE-SWIRLED MARSHMALLOWS

Obviously, you need to know how to make chocolate marshmallows—perfect to lift the spirits or eat on the couch while watching TV. Use the best chocolate you can—they will only be as good as the goodness swirled into them. Add the chocolate at the last minute and mix it in quickly.

INGREDIENTS

1 quantity ingredients for vanilla
   marshmallow mix (see page 10)
2 ounces (50g) semisweet chocolate
1 quantity 50/50 coating
   (see page 10)
2 tablespoons unsweetened
   cocoa

METHOD

Make the marshmallow mix following the method on page 10. While it is having its final whisk, melt the chocolate in a heatproof bowl set over a saucepan of barely simmering water (bain-marie or double-boiler). Be careful to ensure the water isn't touching the bottom of the bowl.

When the chocolate has melted, remove 3–4 large spoonfuls of the marshmallow mix and mix it together with the melted chocolate until smooth and a deep brown color. Pour this mixture into the remaining marshmallow mix and quickly swirl it through. You need to just incorporate it—if you do more than that, the mix will become dense and lose its lightness. Spread into an oiled baking pan and let set.

Mix together the 50/50 coating and cocoa in a medium bowl and dust the marshmallows in it.

Makes 30 marshmallows

VARIATIONS

Instead of using melted chocolate, 3 tablespoons of unsweetened cocoa can be sifted onto a small portion of the marshmallow mix and then swirled through the remaining mix.

Try coating the chocolate marshmallows in other chocolaty treats. Use chocolate sprinkles or chocolate curls created by scraping a knife over the top of a big bar of chocolate.

Add the seeds of a vanilla bean or a small espresso to the mix just before mixing with the chocolate. Both vanilla and coffee will enhance the rich chocolate flavor.

SPICED CHERRY MARSHMALLOWS

If a marshmallow could be a place and time, these would be curled up in front of a log fire after a long leafy fall walk—boots lined up by the back door with a cat purring on your lap. That is the spiced cherry marshmallow. Eat them.

INGREDIENTS

¾ cup (180ml) cherry cordial

2 star anise

1 cinnamon stick

6 cloves

1-inch (2.5cm) piece of fresh
    gingerroot (skin on)

1 quantity ingredients for vanilla
    marshmallow mix (see page 10)

⅓ cup (60g) dried sour cherries,
    coarsely chopped

1 quantity 50/50 coating (see page 10)

METHOD

Pour the cherry cordial into a small saucepan and add the whole spices. Bring the cordial to a boil, then lower the heat to a simmer for 5 minutes. You want the volume to reduce by about half. Remove the whole spices.

Make the marshmallow mix following the method on page 10. Just after adding the sugar syrup to the egg white, pour the reduced spiced cordial onto the mix. Add the gelatin and continue to whisk until thick and voluminous. Mix in the dried cherries then spread into the oiled baking pan.

When set, cut and dust the marshmallows in the usual way with the 50/50 coating.

Makes 30 marshmallows

TOP TIPS

This recipe would work well with other fruit cordial and dried fruit combinations.

Combining the marshmallows with a coating that has a complementary freeze-dried fruit powder mixed through further heightens the fruit tang.

SALTED CARAMEL MARSHMALLOWS

Originating from northern France, the combination of salt and caramel is slowly taking over the world's flavor palate. It works well in a marshmallow because the salt tempers the sweetness. Be brave with the amount of salt and how far you take your caramel. Make 'em dangerous.

INGREDIENTS

For the caramel:
¼ cup (50g) superfine sugar
6 tablespoons (100ml) heavy cream
1 ½ tablespoon (25g) butter
½ teaspoon sea salt flakes

1 quantity ingredients for vanilla
   marshmallow mix (see page 10)
Seeds from 2 vanilla beans
1 quantity 50/50 coating
   (see page 10)

METHOD

Make the caramel first. Measure out the sugar, cream, and butter. It's important to be prepared and in control when making caramel—hot sugar burns like nothing else and you need to be careful.

Place the sugar in a medium saucepan and heat gently over moderate heat. Move the sugar around the saucepan by gently tipping it. It's okay to stir the caramel when using this method if it's melting unevenly. As soon as it has turned a light brown color, pour in the cream and butter. This creates lots of steam and fussing in the saucepan. The caramel will seize and look awful, but keep stirring and the sugar will melt back into the cream. Once it has all melted and is smooth, cook over moderate heat for 2 minutes or until thickened slightly. Add the salt and let cool.

Make the marshmallow mix following the method on page 10. Add the seeds from the vanilla beans at the end after the final whisking. Pour the liquid caramel into the marshmallow mix and fold in briefly. The process of scraping the marshmallow mixture out of the bowl into the baking pan will combine the caramel and marshmallow, so don't overmix. You want the caramel to swirl and ripple through.

Let set overnight, then dust with 50/50 mixture. The caramel makes the marshmallows a little wetter so they will not keep as well.

Makes 30 marshmallows

TOP TIPS

A world of amazing salts are available now, from black volcanic salt to smoked and flavored salts. Experiment to see which you prefer.

LEMON & LIME SHERBET MARSHMALLOWS

The natural sweetness of the marshmallow is tempered by sharp lemon and lime.
What makes these such a refreshing delight is the incorporation of fruit zest and
fizzy sherbet coating—absolutely delicious.

INGREDIENTS

1 quantity ingredients for vanilla
   marshmallow mix (see page 10)
Zest of 1 lemon
Zest of 1 lime, plus extra for decorating
Juice of ½ lemon
Juice of ½ lime
½ cup (50g) confectioners' sugar
1 teaspoon citric acid
   (see Resources, page 144)
1 teaspoon baking soda

METHOD

Make the marshmallow mix following the method on page 10. Incorporate the lemon and lime zest and juice during the final whisking at step 7. The mix will loosen after the juice is added, but whisk it back up to stiff peaks before spreading it into the baking pan to set.

In a small food processor or spice grinder, mix together the confectioners' sugar, citric acid, and baking soda. This should give a fine dusty powder.

Cut the marshmallows to size then dust and decorate with lime zest just before serving. These marshmallows won't keep well once dusted as they become sticky. They are best stored uncut, then cut and dusted at the last minute just before serving.

TOP TIPS

Use a fine Microplane grater (see Resources, page 144) to zest the fruit, and make sure you grate off only the zest, not the pith. This recipe would work as well with orange, grapefruit, or other citrus fruits.

The sherbet coating can be adapted to include flavorings. Try adding freeze-dried fruit or powders to heighten the fruity goodness.

ORANGE, PISTACHIO & RAISIN MARSHMALLOWS

This recipe shows just how versatile marshmallows are, providing a blank canvas for these Middle Eastern and North African flavors—best eaten after a long camel ride with a thick, sweet coffee.

INGREDIENTS

2 tablespoons golden raisins
3 tablespoons (50ml) orange juice
1 quantity ingredients for vanilla
   marshmallow mix (see page 10)
1 teaspoon orange flower water
1 ½ cups (200g) shelled pistachios

METHOD

Soak the golden raisins in the orange juice for about 2 hours until soft and plump.

Make the marshmallow mix following the method on page 10. Add the orange flower water during the final whisking. You may need a little more as the strength of different brands varies. Add according to your taste.

Drain the plump golden raisins and fold into the marshmallow mix. Spread into a greased baking pan or mold and let set.

Finely chop the pistachios in a food processor or spice grinder. Cut and shape the marshmallows, and coat them in the pistachio powder.

Makes 30 marshmallows

TOP TIPS

As with all sweet treats and desserts, these marshmallows work as a consequence of the textural contrasts.

Marshmallows are bouncy and soft. Paired with crunchy nuts and moist raisins, they give your mouth something to think about. That heightens the taste.

Chapter 2

FRUITY

Fresh fruit flavors help to take the edge off the sweetness of a bowl of
marshmallows. Opt for the pure taste of a single fruit—such as apple,
lemon, or melon—or try a cocktail of lemon and ginger, lime and
watermelon, or raspberry and pineapple—there's something for everyone.

LEMON & GINGER MARSHMALLOW CHEESECAKE

This marshmallow exists in the nether world of in-between cake and confectionery. Pleasure or pain? You decide. That's probably overstating it. It's a cross between a cheesecake and a marshmallow—that's better. The textural contrasts here are as important as the flavors. Lovely.

INGREDIENTS
1 quantity ingredients for vanilla marshmallow mix
   (see page 10)
Zest of 2 lemons
½ cup (100g) mascarpone cheese
Few gingersnap cookies

METHOD
Make the marshmallow mix following the method on page 10. As a final step, add the lemon zest and the mascarpone cheese. The fat content of the cheese will cause the marshmallow mix to collapse a little and create something a bit denser. That's okay. Let set.

Break up a few gingersnaps into fine crumbs. Just before serving, cut the marshmallows up and coat them in the crumbs. These are best eaten within a day or two.

Makes about 20 large marshmallows or 8 "cheesecake" slices

TOP TIPS
Obviously, lime or orange zest would work as well, as would other cookies. Pumpkin spice cookies are particularly good here.

APPLE BETTY MARSHMALLOWS

Make sure the apples are tangy and the crumble topping is buttery. The marshmallow gods will do the rest. Eat a spoonful, as required, on rainy Sunday afternoons.

INGREDIENTS

For the crumble topping:
5 tablespoons (75g) butter
¾ cup (75g) almond meal
⅔ cup (75g) all-purpose flour
⅓ cup (75g) brown sugar
Pinch of salt
2 tart apples (Granny Smith, Honeycrisp, or Mutsu are good)
½ teaspoon ground cinnamon
1 quantity ingredients for vanilla marshmallow mix (see page 10)

METHOD

Preheat the oven to 350°F (180°C). For the crumble topping, place the butter, almond meal, flour, brown sugar, and salt in a food processor and mix with the blade attachment until well combined and small lumps start to form. Alternatively, blend the butter into the flour with your fingertips, then add the sugar, almond meal, and salt.

Spread the mixture on a cookie sheet and bake in the oven until golden brown, about 6–8 minutes. Let cool and break up any larger lumps with your fingers.

Peel and core the apples and coarsely chop. Place them in a small saucepan with 1 tablespoon water and heat gently until the apple disintegrates. You need a smooth purée, so if necessary, blend in a food processor or with an immersion blender. Add the cinnamon.

Make the marshmallow mix following the method on page 10, and at step 6, add the apple purée.

Pour the marshmallow mix into a greased baking pan and level the surface with an offset spatula. Sprinkle the crumble mix over the top and press it into the surface to create an even crust.

Let set overnight, then serve spoonfuls, or cut into small ovals or circles to recreate the appearance of an apple betty.

Makes 30 large marshmallows

FRUIT SALAD SKEWERS

When I was at school, the seniors sold snacks like "fruit salad" and "black Jack" flavored candies for a few cents each. My fondness for those candies remains fierce.

INGREDIENTS

2 quantities ingredients for vanilla
marshmallow mix (see page 10)
Pineapple flavoring (see tips below)
½ cup (100g) raspberry purée
Yellow and pink food coloring (optional)
½ cup (50g) raspberry powder
(optional, see Resources, page 144)
½ cup (50g) pineapple powder
(optional, see Resources, page 144)
2 quantities 50/50 coating
(optional, see page 10)

30 bamboo skewers, to serve

METHOD

Make 2 batches of plain marshmallow mix following the method on page 10. At step 6, add the pineapple flavoring and yellow food coloring (if using) to one batch, and the raspberry purée and pink food coloring (if using) to the second batch.

Let marshmallow set, then cut into even and matching cubes. Dust with the matching fruit powder, if desired, or use the basic 50/50 coating mix. The marshmallows will keep longer if dusted in the cornstarch/confectioners' sugar mix, but the fruit powder will heighten the taste.

Spear 2 marshmallows, one of each flavor, on each bamboo skewer and serve.

Makes 30 skewers

TOP TIPS

Some fruits contain an enzyme that breaks down the proteins in gelatin. These include pineapple, papaya, kiwi, and, supposedly, melon, so a natural flavoring extract needs to be used instead. However, the recipe for melon marshmallows (see page 35) works well, as the process of puréeing the fruit denatures the enzyme.

The ½ cup of fruit purée in this recipe can be replaced easily with different store-bought or homemade purées.

BANOFFEE MARSHMALLOWS

Sweet bananas meet sweet caramel, meet sweet marshmallows. Surely the healthy fruit content balances out the less-than-healthy sugars in this case?

INGREDIENTS

For the caramel:
6 tablespoons (100ml) heavy cream
1 ½ tablespoons (20g) butter
¼ cup (50g) superfine sugar
½ teaspoon sea salt

1 banana
Squeeze of lemon juice
1 quantity ingredients for vanilla
   marshmallow mix (see page 10)
1 quantity 50/50 coating (see page 10)

METHOD

First make the caramel. Measure out the cream and butter to have them ready. Place the superfine sugar in a medium saucepan and warm gently. You'll need to stand over the pan and keep an eye on it the whole time while the sugar caramelizes. Gently swirl the saucepan to help the sugar melt evenly. When the sugar has reached an even light brown color, add the cream and butter. The caramel will solidify, but have faith and keep stirring. The sugar will melt back into the cream and butter. Keep stirring until the caramel is smooth and thickened slightly. This should take 2–3 minutes. Add the salt and let cool.

Peel the banana and purée in a food processor. Add a squeeze of lemon juice to stop the purée from oxidizing and turning brown.

Make the marshmallow mix following the method on page 10, and add the banana purée at step 6. Just before tipping the marshmallow mix out into a baking pan to set, add the caramel and swirl carefully through the mix. Let set. The caramel and banana in this mix will give a softer marshmallow, so cut and dust with the 50/50 coating carefully. Best eaten within a couple of days.

Makes 30 large marshmallows

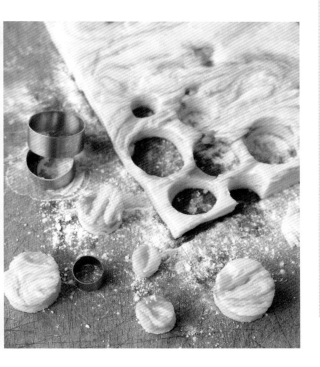

LIME MARSHMALLOW & GRILLED WATERMELON FRUIT KABOBS

Pairing fresh fruit with homemade marshmallows is a joy. The trick here is to cut the marshmallows and cubes of watermelon to the same size. If you haven't tried grilling watermelon before, you must—it's a revelation.

INGREDIENTS

1 quantity ingredients for vanilla
  marshmallow mix (see page 10)
Juice and zest of 2 limes
½ watermelon

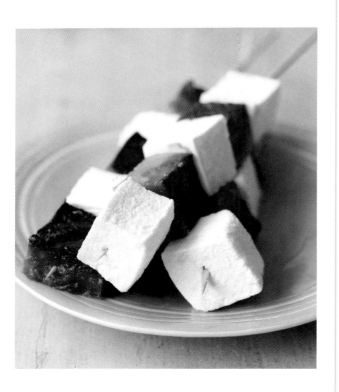

METHOD

Make the marshmallow mix following the method on page 10, and add the lime zest and juice at step 6. Let the marshmallow set.

Remove the skin from the watermelon and cut the marshmallows and melon into identical-size cubes.

Light up your grill or place a ridged skillet over high heat. Chargrill the melon on all sides.

When the melon is ready, divide the marshmallow and melon cubes among eight skewers. Serve immediately.

Makes 8 kabobs

TIP

Don't grill the marshmallows with the melon from the start. The melon takes a while to cook, and the marshmallows will have fallen off the grill by the time it's ready.

LEMON CURD-STUFFED VANILLA MARSHMALLOWS

This recipe is a good excuse to immerse yourself in the world of cake and chocolate molds. Flexible silicone molds are best for this recipe. There's an extraordinary range available now. These work best in small (about 1 ½ inches/3.75cm diameter) demispheres or even mini muffin pans.

INGREDIENTS

For the lemon curd:
4 lemons
12 egg yolks
1 cup (200g) superfine sugar
14 tablespoons (200g)
    butter, melted

1 tablespoon vegetable oil
1 quantity 50/50 coating
(see page 10)
1 quantity ingredients for
    vanilla marshmallow mix
    (see page 10)

METHOD

First make the lemon curd. Zest and juice the lemons and place in a small saucepan on moderate heat. Reduce the juice by half and let cool in the saucepan. Combine the egg yolks and sugar in a small bowl then add the melted butter. Pour the reduced lemon juice through a small fine strainer (to remove the zest) into the egg, sugar, and butter mixture. Pour the mixture into a medium saucepan and warm over gentle heat until it's transformed from thin and glossy to thick and matt. Let cool.

Brush your molds lightly with the vegetable oil and then dust lightly with a little of the 50/50 confectioners' sugar/cornstarch mix.

Make the marshmallow mix following the method on page 10. Pipe or carefully spoon half of the marshmallow mix into the bottom of the molds.

Fill a pastry bag with the cooled lemon curd and pipe a small amount into the center of each marshmallow mold. Fill the rest of each mold with the remaining marshmallow mix and smooth off the top. Dust the tops of the molds with the 50/50 coating and let set.

Makes 30 large marshmallows

TOP TIPS

You could use store-bought lemon curd here although it's never as good as homemade. The amounts here will give you leftover curd to spread on toast. The same recipe works well with lime or even passion fruit juice.

Decorate the tops of these marshmallows with a sprinkling of lemon sugar: add the zest of 1 lemon to ½ cup superfine sugar and blend in a food processor for a few seconds. Store in an airtight container.

MARSHMALLOW DAIFUKU(ISH)

Inspired by the Japanese confection daifuku, in which mochi (a sweet, glutinous rice cake) is wrapped around fruit or red bean paste. Here the sweet marshmallow is balanced by the fresh fruity core. Use all bean paste, or all fruit, or a mixture of both.

INGREDIENTS

Sweet red bean paste (anko) (see tip below) and/or 15–30 pieces fresh fruit (small, firm fruit, such as strawberries and grapes, work best here)
1 quantity ingredients for vanilla marshmallow mix (see page 10)
1 quantity 50/50 coating, plus extra confectioners' sugar for dusting (see page 10)

METHOD

Dust your hands and work surface with confectioners' sugar and roll 15–30 small (¾-inch/2cm) balls from the anko bean paste. Place them in the refrigerator to firm up.

Make the marshmallow mix following the method on page 10 but keep the mix relatively loose and runny. You need to be able to coat the fruit or bean paste easily with it. If the mix is stiff, it will be difficult to use as a coating.

Dust a cookie sheet with the 50/50 coating.

Push a toothpick into the bean paste ball or a piece of fruit and delicately dunk into the marshmallow mix. Swirl it around until well coated. Push the fruit- or bean paste-covered ball off the toothpick onto the dusted cookie sheet. Dust the tops of the marshmallow-covered balls of goodness with more sugar/cornstarch mix.

These need to be eaten on the day they are made as the water content of the fruit and/or bean paste will soften the marshmallow mix.

Makes 30 marshmallows

TIP

Bean paste can be bought in 1-pound (450g) packages. It is available online or in Asian supermarkets. It can be made at home from adzuki beans, water, and sugar. It's easy enough to make but takes a while.

MELON MARSHMALLOWS

The perfume and scent of the melon comes through really well in this one, but you need a properly ripe melon. Most varieties work well, but not watermelon. Galia or honeydew melons are my favorite. With some slices of top-quality ham, or preferably prosciutto, these make a great canapé.

INGREDIENTS

1 quantity ingredients for vanilla
 marshmallow mix (see page 10)
Large slice of ripe melon
 (about 6 ounces/175g)
Few slices of prosciutto or ham (optional)

METHOD

Scoop out the flesh from the melon and discard the skin. Blend the flesh to a purée in a food processor or press the flesh through a fine strainer with the back of a spoon. You need ½ cup purée.

Make the marshmallow mix following the method on page 10. Add the melon purée as part of step 6.

Let set and cut into generous cubes. Wrap the cubes in small rectangles of prosciutto if desired.

Makes about 30 large marshmallows

ROSE PETAL MARSHMALLOWS

Fragrant, elegant, and delightful. These marshmallows are delicately scented with both rose water and crystallized rose petals—perfect after a hard day shopping in your local mall.

INGREDIENTS

4 tablespoons crystallized rose petals
1 quantity ingredients for vanilla
    marshmallow mix (see page 10)
About 1 teaspoon rose water
Natural pink food coloring
1 quantity 50/50 coating (see page 10)
Fresh rose petals, for decorating

METHOD

Using a mortar and pestle, crush the rose petals into smaller fragments about $\frac{1}{16}$–$\frac{1}{8}$ inch (1–3mm) in size.

Make the marshmallow mix following the method on page 10. Add the rose water during the final whisking stage. The potency of rose water differs remarkably—some brands will need only a few drops, some a tablespoon. Go easy, and taste after each addition until you've got a flavor you enjoy. Stop whisking and fold in the crushed crystallized rose petals.

Scrape out the marshmallow mix into a lightly greased baking pan. Drip small drops of the food coloring on top of the mix and swirl through with the end of a spoon or toothpick. Let set, then dust with the 50/50 coating. Cut into cubes.

Serve the marshmallows decorated with fresh rose petals.

Makes 30 large marshmallows

EARL GREY & LEMON MARSHMALLOWS

Infusing tea into marshmallows is a quick and clever way of adding refined and intriguing flavors. The principle behind this recipe would work for any flavor of tea. It also works well for botanical flavors such as hibiscus, jasmine, and chamomile.

INGREDIENTS

2 tablespoons loose-leaf Earl Grey tea
1 quantity 50/50 coating (see page 10)
1 quantity ingredients for vanilla
  marshmallow mix (see page 10)
Zest of 1 lemon
Juice of ½ lemon

METHOD

Divide the tea leaves into two and finely grind one portion in a spice grinder. Place in a small bowl and mix with three-quarters of the 50/50 coating. This will be the marshmallow coating.

Place the remaining tablespoon of tea in a cup and pour over ½ cup hot water. Infuse for 5 minutes. Strain the liquid through a fine strainer.

Make the marshmallow mix following the method on page 10, but use 4 tablespoons of the strained tea in place of the water that is added to the sugar to make the sugar syrup.

Add the lemon zest and juice during the final whisking stage. Scrape the marshmallow mix into a lightly greased baking pan. Let set, then cut and dust with the tea coating.

Makes 30 large marshmallows

Chapter 3

CHOCOLATE

If you're one of those people who always succumbs to a square of chocolate, imagine how hard it is to say "no" to a chocolate marshmallow. Whether the marshmallows are mixed with chocolate before setting, coated in it, or made up of several chocolate layers, resistance is useless.

EGG-FREE CHOCOLATE & HAZELNUT MARSHMALLOWS ON STICKS

Marshmallow mix is easily shaped into fun shapes and sizes. This recipe proves once again that everything tastes better when eaten off a stick. Consider chargrilling, drizzling in hot chocolate sauce, or even having bizarre candy-based sword fights. En garde!

INGREDIENTS

1 teaspoon vegetable oil
1 quantity ingredients for egg-free
    marshmallow mix (see page 12)
3 ounces (75g) semisweet
    chocolate, coarsely chopped
1 ½ cups (200g) shelled
    hazelnuts, toasted

Acetate sheets (see method and
    Resources, page 144)
Adhesive tape
12 long lollipop or cake pop sticks
Disposable pastry bag

METHOD

Create the molds by shaping the acetate sheets into cylinders. Cut rectangles of acetate 4 x 5 ½ inches (10 x 14cm). Join the shorter sides with adhesive tape, overlapping them by ½ inch (1.25cm). Lightly grease the cylinders with vegetable oil and place on a greased cookie sheet.

Melt the chocolate in a heatproof bowl set over a saucepan of barely simmering water (bain-marie or double-boiler). Be careful to ensure the water isn't touching the bottom of the bowl.

Make the egg-free marshmallow mix and add the melted chocolate after the final mixing stage. Gently stir in the chocolate just enough to combine.

Scrape the marshmallow mix into a pastry bag and pipe into the acetate cylinders. Let set for about 30 minutes, then push in the lollipop sticks. Make sure the mix is stiff enough to hold the stick vertically. Let the marshmallows finish setting in the molds.

Finely chop the hazelnuts. Peel off the acetate strips from the marshmallows. They should peel away relatively easily, but it may be necessary to use a small knife or spatula to loosen the acetate.

Roll the marshmallows in the chopped hazelnuts and serve.

Makes 12 sticks

EGG-FREE TRIPLE CHOCOLATE LAYERED MARSHMALLOWS

These are as pretty as they are tasty.

INGREDIENTS

1 teaspoon vegetable oil

2 quantities ingredients for egg-free marshmallow mix (see page 12)

2 ounces (60g) white chocolate

2 ounces (60g) milk chocolate

2 ounces (60g) semisweet chocolate

1 quantity 50/50 coating (see page 10)

1 tablespoon unsweetened cocoa

METHOD

Lightly grease a 6-inch (15cm) square cake pan with the oil.

Chop each of the types of chocolate and place in three separate small heatproof bowls. In turn, place the bowls over a small saucepan of barely simmering water (bain-marie or double-boiler) and let the chocolate melt. Remove from the saucepan and keep to one side. If the chocolate starts to set before the marshmallow mix is ready, then place them back on top of the saucepan for about 30 seconds.

Make a double-quantity egg-free marshmallow mix (see page 12). When whisking up the mix to its final volume, ensure you have everything ready to mix and layer the marshmallow. Adding chocolate directly to the mix will immediately stiffen it up, so you need to work quickly.

Divide the marshmallow mix among three bowls. Add the white chocolate to one of the bowls. Quickly mix the chocolate through with a spatula and then immediately spread the mix into the base of the cake pan. Put the cake pan into the refrigerator briefly. Add the milk chocolate to the second bowl of the marshmallow mix and spread that on top of the white chocolate layer. Return the pan to the refrigerator while you prepare the next layer. Add the semisweet chocolate to the final third of the mix and spread over the top of the milk chocolate layer. Let set, then cut. Mix the 50/50 coating with the cocoa and then use to dust the marshmallows.

Makes 30–40 large marshmallows

TOP TIPS

This recipe uses the egg-free variation of the marshmallow mix because chocolate causes the classic egg white version to collapse.

A small offset spatula is an invaluable tool to spread even layers in the pan.

BAILEYS MARSHMALLOW CHOCOLATE HAZELNUT CUPS

Readymade chocolate cups are a wonderful pantry standby. Quickly fill with mousse or fruit, and—tah-dah—you're a goddess in the kitchen. Filled with boozy and runny Baileys marshmallows, they make a very grown-up canapé or petit four.

INGREDIENTS

½ quantity ingredients for vanilla marshmallow mix (see page 10)
6 tablespoons (100ml) Baileys liqueur
15 chocolate cups (see tips below)
⅔ cup (100g) shelled whole hazelnuts

METHOD

Make the marshmallow mix following the method on page 10. After the final whisking, add the Baileys. Whisk until just combined and smooth.

Divide the mix among the readymade chocolate cups and place in the refrigerator to set.

Preheat the oven to 350°F (180°C). Spread the whole hazelnuts on a cookie sheet and toast in the oven for 8–10 minutes or until golden brown. Coarsely chop the nuts and sprinkle on top of the marshmallow. Serve.

Makes 15 cups

TOP TIPS

Making your own chocolate cups isn't hard. All you require is a suitable mold. Something rigid—polycarbonate works best. Then you fill the molds with melted chocolate.

Molds for chocolate cups come in many sizes. Something approximately 1 ½–2 inches (4–5cm) in diameter and depth works well. There are lots of designs available (see Resources, page 144), but many are only available in large quantities, so choose wisely.

MINT CHOCOLATE CHIP MARSHMALLOWS

The use of fresh mint as a vibrant green decoration lifts these treats and balances the rich chocolate.

INGREDIENTS

1 quantity ingredients for
   vanilla marshmallow mix
   (see page 10)
Peppermint flavoring
Natural green food coloring
⅔ cup (100g) semisweet
   chocolate chips
Large handful of fresh
   mint leaves
3 tablespoons superfine sugar
1 quantity 50/50 coating
   (see page 10)

METHOD

Make the marshmallow mix following the method on page 10. At Step 6, add peppermint flavoring to your own preference, tasting after every 4–5 drops. Add drops of food coloring until you have a pale green color. After the final whisking, stir in the chocolate chips. Spread the marshmallow mix into a greased baking pan and let set. Blend the mint leaves and superfine sugar together in a food processor until you have bright green mint sugar.

When the marshmallow has set, cut into cubes and dust with 50/50 coating mix.

Just before serving, dampen one side of each marshmallow by pressing it against a damp cloth. Then press the dampened side into the mint sugar to coat and arrange on a plate, mint coating on top.

Makes 30 marshmallows

CHOCOLATE-COATED MARSHMALLOWS

What's better than a marshmallow? A chocolate-coated marshmallow. Coating things in chocolate can be both gourmet food art and guilty snack food pleasure.

INGREDIENTS

8 ounces (225g) dark chocolate
1 quantity vanilla marshmallows
   (see page 10)
Decorations such as crystallized
   violets, vanilla sugar, or
   freeze-dried raspberries

METHOD

Melt the dark chocolate in a heatproof bowl set over a saucepan of barely simmering water (bain-marie or double-boiler), place a marshmallow on a fork, dip in the chocolate, then leave on wax paper until set. Decorate the chocolates to indicate the flavor of the marshmallow: crystallized violets, vanilla sugar, freeze-dried raspberries, etc.

HOT CHOCOLATE WITH INDIAN CHAI SPICED MARSHMALLOWS

Naturally, hot chocolate and marshmallows are best friends, but this recipe maximizes that combo. Inspired by Indian chai spiced tea, these marshmallows melt into the chocolate to give up their fragrant and alluring charm.

INGREDIENTS

1 star anise
Seeds from 4 cardamom pods
½ cinnamon stick
4 black peppercorns
2 allspice berries
2 cloves
½ teaspoon ground ginger
1 quantity ingredients for vanilla
    marshmallow mix (see page 10)
1 quantity 50/50 coating (see page 10)

FOR THE HOT CHOCOLATE:

3 ½ ounces (100g) semisweet chocolate
½ tablespoon cornstarch
1 tablespoon milk powder
About 1 ¼ cups (300ml) milk

METHOD

Place all the whole spices in a spice grinder and grind until fine. Pass through a fine strainer to ensure there are no larger pieces. Add the ground ginger to the spice mixture.

Make the marshmallow mix following the method on page 10 and add in the ground spices during the final whisking stage.

Scrape the marshmallow mix into a lightly oiled baking pan and let set.

Cut the marshmallows. As these are going to be melted, they look better cut into interesting shapes with cookie cutters—stars, moons, circles, etc. Dust the marshmallow shapes with the 50/50 coating mix.

Make the hot chocolate by finely chopping the chocolate, preferably using a food processor. Mix in the cornstarch and milk powder.

For a rich espresso-like hot chocolate, warm the chocolate mix gently in a pan with the milk. Stir continuously until smooth. For a lighter, thinner drink use more milk.

Drop a few marshmallows into the chocolate and enjoy.

Serves 4

CHOCOLATE, CHILI & LIME MARSHMALLOWS

A great variation for the recipe to the right is to add in lime. The combination of chili and lime is pert and sparky—a marshmallow to take notice of.

Follow the recipe on the right but add in the zest and juice of 1 lime with the melted chocolate and chopped chili.

CHOCOLATE CHIPOTLE CHILI MARSHMALLOWS

The deep smokiness of the chilis works wonderfully with the rich chocolate.

INGREDIENTS

5 dried chipotle chilis
5 sheets (¼ ounce) platinum-strength leaf gelatin
1 ⅓ cups (280g) superfine sugar
1 ½ tablespoons (25ml) glucose syrup
2 ½ ounces (70g) semisweet chocolate
½ quantity 50/50 coating (see page 10)
1 tablespoon unsweetened cocoa

METHOD

Soak the chilis in ¾ cup (200ml) cold water for at least 30 minutes. They need to have softened, and the water needs to infuse with the chili flavor. Remove the chilis but keep the water. Finely chop the chilis.

Soak the gelatin sheets in the chili-infused water until soft. Place the softened gelatin in a small saucepan with 2 tablespoons of the chili water and melt the gelatin over very low heat. Pour the melted gelatin into the bowl of a free-standing mixer and whisk for 2 minutes until frothy.

Mix together the sugar, glucose syrup, and 4 tablespoons of the reserved chili water in a small saucepan. Heat gently until it registers 250°F (120°C) on a digital candy thermometer, then pour onto the gelatin while still whisking.

Melt the chocolate in a heatproof bowl set over a saucepan of barely simmering water (bain-marie or double-boiler). Be careful to ensure the water isn't touching the bottom of the bowl.

Once the marshmallow mix has reached soft peaks, add the finely chopped chili and then the melted chocolate. Continue whisking the mix until the chocolate is just combined. Scrape the marshmallow mixture out of the bowl into an oiled baking pan, and let set. Mix the 50/50 coating with the cocoa. Cut and dust the marshmallows with 50/50 coating mix.

Makes 20 (1 ¼-inch/3cm) marshmallow cubes

TIP

If you're feeling ridiculously brave, ½ teaspoon of chili powder could be added to the 50/50 coating. Alternatively, try adding a few drops of your favorite hot sauce during the final whisking.

COCONUT, PASSION FRUIT & MILK CHOCOLATE MARSHMALLOWS

Bright and zesty passion fruit combines perfectly with milk chocolate and coconut—a tropical cocktail coated in chocolate.

INGREDIENTS

3 passion fruit
1 quantity ingredients for vanilla
    marshmallow mix (see page 10)
1 cup (100g) shredded coconut
5 ounces (150g) milk chocolate

METHOD

Juice the passion fruit. Remove the seeds if you prefer, but hidden within the marshmallow, they make a great textural contrast. However, these marshmallows won't store well with the seeds in.

Make the marshmallow mix following the method on page 10, and add the passion fruit juice during the final stage of whisking.

Spread the marshmallow mix into an oiled baking pan and let set. Cut into cubes and dust with the shredded coconut.

Melt the chocolate in a heatproof bowl set over a saucepan of barely simmering water (bain-marie or double-boiler). Be careful to ensure the water isn't touching the bottom of the bowl.

Line a cookie sheet with wax paper. Dip one side of each marshmallow into the melted chocolate. Let the excess chocolate drip off, then place the marshmallows on the wax paper to set, chocolate side up.

Makes 30 large marshmallows

Chapter 4

EXTRAORDINARY

A twist on the traditional, these marshmallows will delight your
taste buds with their unexpected flavor combinations. From the
timeless pairings of peanut butter and jelly, or lavender and honey, to
the Asian-inspired pandan and coconut or saffron and cardamom,
find something new here.

LAVENDER & HONEY MARSHMALLOWS

These are as fresh and floral as a traditional New England garden party. Different types of honey will impart subtly different flavor tones. I favor set honey and freshly picked lavender. Eat outside with a cup of hot tea.

INGREDIENTS

5 sheets (¼ ounce/8g) platinum-strength
   leaf gelatin
1 egg white (1 ¼ ounces/35g)
1 cup (280g) honey
1 ½ tablespoons (25ml) glucose syrup
Lavender extract or fresh lavender flowers
   (angustifolia variety)
1 quantity 50/50 coating (see page 10)

METHOD

Make the marshmallow mix following
the method on page 10, replacing the
superfine sugar with the honey and
using only 2 tablespoons (30ml) water
for the syrup.

Add the lavender flavoring at step 6.
If using lavender flowers, pick the small
buds carefully from the stems. In both
cases, go easy when adding the lavender;
there is a fine line between delicious and
as overpowering as Grandma's underwear-
drawer liners. You've been warned.

Scrape the mix into a lightly oiled baking pan
and let set. Cut and dust with the 50/50
coating mix. Decorating with a few fresh
lavender buds would be perfect.

Makes 30 large marshmallows

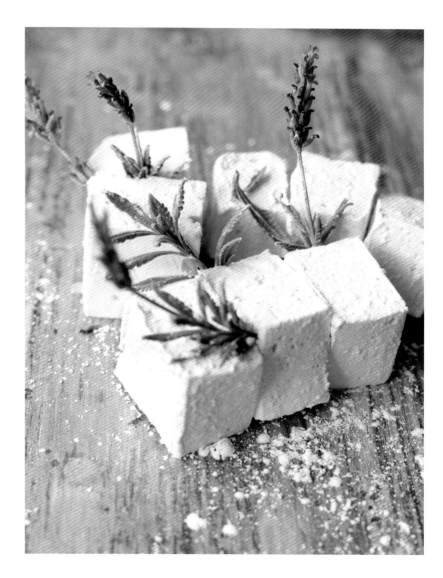

RASPBERRY, ROSE & LYCHEE MARSHMALLOWS

These are inspired by the Pierre Hermé classic flavor combination in his Ispahan macarons. They are transcendentally beautifully delicious and scrumptious.

INGREDIENTS

¾ cup (100g) raspberries to give
¼ cup (60g) raspberry purée
5 ounces (150g) lychees to give
¼ cup (60g) lychee purée
(see tips below)
1 teaspoon vegetable oil
Natural pink food coloring
½ teaspoon rose water

3 quantities vanilla marshmallow mix
using the following quantities for
each batch:
4 sheets (⅛ ounce/5g) platinum-
strength leaf gelatin
1 small egg white (¾ ounce/20g)
¾ cup (170g) superfine sugar
1 tablespoon (15ml) glucose syrup
3 tablespoons (40ml) water

2 quantities 50/50 coating
(see page 10)

METHOD

This recipe involves making and flavoring three batches of marshmallow. Make the purées first. Blend the raspberries in a food processor until smooth. Pass through a fine strainer to remove the seeds. Repeat for the lychees. Oil an 8-inch (20cm) square cake pan with the vegetable oil.

Make the raspberry-flavored marshmallow, following the method on page 10. Add the purée at the final stage after whisking, then whisk for 3–4 minutes to regain some of the volume. Add a few drops of food coloring. Spread evenly into the oiled pan. Put in the refrigerator to set.

Make up another batch of vanilla marshmallow and add the rose water to flavor together with 2 tablespoons (30ml) water to thin the mix to a similar consistency to the raspberry layer. Add pink coloring to give a lighter shade than the raspberry. Spread evenly onto the raspberry layer. Return to the refrigerator to set.

Make the lychee layer in the same way as the raspberry layer. Leave it white. Let set. Cut and dust with the 50/50 coating mixture.

Makes 40 large marshmallows

TIPS

For a boozy version, a tablespoon of raspberry liqueur (Chambord), rose liqueur, or lychee liqueur (Kwai Feh) can be added to each batch of marshmallow instead of the fruit purées and rose water.

Lychee purée can be found in stores in 2-pound (900g) quantities. Blending and straining canned lychees works well, or use lychee juice from a carton.

PANDAN & COCONUT MARSHMALLOWS

Pandan leaf is used in Thai and Southeast Asian desserts. It gives these marshmallows a complex, vanilla popcorn-like taste. The coconut dusting adds texture and boosts their nutty flavor.

INGREDIENTS

1 quantity ingredients for vanilla
  marshmallow mix (see page 10)
1 teaspoon pandan extract (see tip below)
Natural green food coloring
1 cup (100g) shredded coconut

METHOD

Make the plain marshmallow mix following the method on page 10. After the final whisking, add the pandan extract and a few drops of the green coloring to give a pale green appearance. Scrape the mix into a lightly oiled baking pan.

Place the shredded coconut in a dry skillet over moderate heat and toast until it turns golden brown and a warm nutty aroma fills the kitchen.

When the marshmallow has set, cut to shape and coat in the toasted coconut.

Makes 30 large marshmallows

TIP

Pandan extract can be bought from Asian supermarkets and stores. It's incredible stuff and can be used to flavor sponge cake, custards, and other desserts. Buy some.

BLACK CURRANT & VIOLET MARSHMALLOWS

There is no better sweet flavor combination than sharp zesty black currants and heady floral violets. Decorated with whole crystallized violets, these make an opulent treat.

INGREDIENTS

1 ⅓ cups (150g) black currants
1 quantity ingredients for vanilla marshmallow mix
    (see page 10)
Violet flavoring
1 quantity 50/50 coating (see page 10)
Crystallized violets

METHOD

Place the black currants in a food processor and blend until smooth. You will need ½ cup black currant purée.

Make up the plain marshmallow mix following the method on page 10, adding the black currant purée at step 6. Add a few drops of violet flavoring, tasting as you go until you have the balance you desire. The mixture will have loosened a lot with the addition of the purée, so whisk again for another 4–5 minutes.

Scrape the mix into a lightly oiled baking pan.

When the marshmallow has set, cut and dust with plain 50/50 coating. Decorate with crystallized violets.

Makes 30 large marshmallows

BROWN SUGAR & GINGER MARSHMALLOWS

What's brilliant about these is that the natural taste of the brown sugar shines through. The caramel molasses pairs perfectly with the ginger. They make the ideal holiday stocking stuffer.

INGREDIENTS

For the marshmallow:
2 pieces stem ginger in syrup
1 teaspoon vegetable oil
5 sheets (¼ ounce/8g) platinum-strength
   leaf gelatin
1 egg white (1 ¼ ounces/35g)
1 ⅓ cups (280g) light brown sugar
1 ½ tablespoons (25ml) glucose syrup
3 tablespoons (60ml) water

FOR THE COATING:

1 quantity 50/50 coating (see page 10)
½ teaspoon ground ginger

METHOD

Chop the stem ginger into pieces no bigger than ⅛–¼ inch (3–6mm). Oil a baking pan with the vegetable oil.

Make the marshmallow mix following the method on page 10, replacing the superfine sugar with the brown sugar.

Stir through the pieces of stem ginger at the last stage before scraping the marshmallow mix out into the greased baking pan to set.

Combine the 50/50 coating and ground ginger in a small bowl. Once the marshmallow has set, cut and dust with the coating.

Makes 30 large marshmallows

PBJ MARSHMALLOWS

Peanut butter and jelly works in any snack: sandwich, cake, candy, and definitely in a marshmallow. In this recipe, the peanut butter is used in its purest form—warmed and drizzled.

INGREDIENTS

¾ cup (100g) fresh raspberries
1 quantity ingredients for vanilla marshmallow mix (see page 10)
¼ ounce (10g) freeze-dried raspberries
   (available in supermarkets and online)
½ quantity 50/50 coating (see page 10)
⅔ cup (150g) smooth peanut butter

METHOD

Place the raspberries in a food processor and blend until smooth. Pass through a fine strainer to remove the seeds.

Make the marshmallow mix following the method on page 10. Add the raspberry purée to the mix at Step 6. Whisk again for 4–5 minutes until the volume has returned. Add half the freeze-dried raspberries, stir through, then scrape out into a lightly oiled baking pan and let set.

Blend the remaining freeze-dried raspberries with the 50/50 coating mix. Once the marshmallow has set, cut and dust with the raspberry coating. Warm the peanut butter in a saucepan and drizzle over the marshmallows just before serving.

Makes 30 large marshmallows

TIP

These can be made as a two-layered marshmallow, one layer being the raspberry recipe above and the second layer being a plain mix flavored with 6 tablespoons peanut butter. However, the peanut butter will make its layer rather dense.

COLA MARSHMALLOWS

This recipe is a good example of utilizing what is available in supermarket aisles. Store-bought cola soda flavoring paired with a sherbet coating recreates the beverage.

INGREDIENTS

1 quantity ingredients for
    vanilla marshmallow mix
    (see page 10)
¼ cup (50g) cola soda flavoring
½ cup (50g) confectioners'
    sugar
1 teaspoon citric acid
    (see Resources, page 144)
1 teaspoon baking soda

METHOD

Make the marshmallow mix following the method on page 10. Add the cola flavoring at Step 6, then whisk back to firm peaks and maximum volume. Scrape into a lightly oiled baking pan and let set.

Place the confectioners' sugar, citric acid, and baking soda in a food processor and blend until you have a fine sherbet powder. Dust the marshmallows with the sherbet just before serving as the mix will make the marshmallows become damp over time.

Makes 30 large marshmallows

MILK & COOKIES MARSHMALLOWS

It's kind of clever just how much these taste of milk despite there only being a relatively small amount of milk in them. Covered in cookie crumbs, they are really rather tasty.

INGREDIENTS

1 quantity ingredients for
    vanilla marshmallow mix
    (see page 10)
1 ¼ cups (300ml) milk
Few of your favorite cookies,
    crumbled—Oreos are
    particularly good here

METHOD

Make the marshmallow mix following the method on page 10, but replace the 4 tablespoons water in the sugar syrup with 4 tablespoons milk, and soak the gelatin sheets in the remaining milk.

When the milk and sugar syrup is added to the egg white, the mix will collapse. Keep whisking, and the softened gelatin will start to cause the volume to rise. Scrape the marshmallow mix into a lightly oiled baking pan. While the marshmallow is still warm and tacky, sprinkle with the cookie crumbs. Let set, then cut into pieces.

Makes 30 marshmallows

ESPRESSO MARSHMALLOWS

Elegant and understated. These look best as perfect cubes presented with coffee at the end of a meal with good friends. Good coffee = good marshmallow.

INGREDIENTS

For the marshmallow:
5 sheets (¼ ounce/8g) platinum-strength leaf gelatin
⅔ cup (150ml) cold espresso (or strong coffee)
1 egg white (1 ¼ ounces/35g)
1 ¼ cups (280g) superfine sugar
1 ½ tablespoons (25ml) glucose syrup

For the coating:
1 quantity 50/50 coating (see page 10)
1 ½ tablespoons (10g) unsweetened cocoa

METHOD

Make the marshmallow mix following the method on page 10, but soak the gelatin sheets in the espresso instead of water to soften. You'll need to place the gelatin in a shallow dish or bowl so the espresso completely covers it.

At step 6 of the method, add 4 tablespoons of the espresso to the mix. The mix will loosen a little, so you'll need to bring it back up to peak volume with another 4–5 minutes whisking.

Scrape the mix into a lightly oiled baking pan and let set.

Combine the confectioners' sugar, cornstarch, and cocoa in a small bowl. Once the marshmallow has set, cut and dust with the cocoa mixture.

Makes 30 large marshmallows

TIPS

These marshmallows also work well on top of a cup of hot chocolate. Another coffee marshmallow delight can be achieved by putting one vanilla marshmallow in the bottom of a coffee cup and pouring hot coffee over the top.

MOCHA MARSHMALLOWS

An easy variation of the espresso recipe above, is with the addition of 3 ½ ounces (100g) semisweet chocolate. The joy of this is that the chocolate remains distinct from the marshmallow and forms tiny strata of solid chocolate.

Melt the chocolate in a heatproof bowl set over a saucepan of barely simmering water (bain-marie or double-boiler). Just before scraping out and setting the espresso marshmallow, add the melted chocolate and fold it in for 2–3 seconds. Don't fully incorporate it—you want a rippled effect.

Scrape out the marshmallow mix and let set.

SALTED BUTTERED POPCORN MARSHMALLOWS

It's your favorite movie treat in a marshmallow. This marshmallow works particularly well because of the texture contrast between the crispy popcorn and buttery marshmallow beneath.

INGREDIENTS

¼ cup (50g) popping corn
10 tablespoons (150g) butter
½ teaspoon plain table salt
1 tablespoon vegetable oil
1 quantity ingredients for vanilla
    marshmallow mix (see page 10)

METHOD

First, pop your corn. Once the popping gets going, turn the heat off and leave the corn to do its stuff. Melt half the butter. Toss the popcorn in the melted butter with a few pinches of salt and let cool.

Line a baking pan with wax or silicone paper, then oil the paper with the vegetable oil.

Make the marshmallow mix following the method on page 10. Add ¼ teaspoon salt into the mix at step 6. Scrape out of the mixing bowl and spread into the prepared baking pan. Let the marshmallows cool and set.

Place the cooled butter-covered popcorn in a food processor and blend to small pieces. Melt the remaining butter. Cut up the marshmallow into pieces and coat in the melted butter, then toss in the crushed popcorn.

Makes 30 large marshmallows

GOLD, SAFFRON & CARDAMOM MARSHMALLOWS

Perhaps not an everyday treat, but this recipe illustrates how marshmallows can be elevated to exclusive and cultured delights.

INGREDIENTS

1 tablespoon vegetable oil
6 cardamom pods
Pinch of saffron (see Resources, page 144)
1 quantity ingredients for vanilla marshmallow mix (see page 10)
1 quantity 50/50 coating (see page 10)
Gold leaf—as much as you can afford! (each marshmallow needs
   approximately 1 sheet)

METHOD

Line a baking pan with wax or silicone paper, then oil the paper with vegetable oil. Crush the cardamom pods and the seeds within them, and place in a small saucepan with 3 tablespoons water. Bring just to a boil, then remove from the heat and let the cardamom infuse for 30 minutes. Pass the liquid through a fine strainer. Add the saffron strands, and let them infuse and color the water.

Make the marshmallow mix following the method on page 10. Add the cardamom- and saffron-infused water at Step 6, then whisk until the mixture forms stiff peaks and reaches maximum volume. Scrape into the prepared baking pan. Let set, then cut into cubes.

Dust the cubes with 50/50 mix, and place a piece of gold leaf on the top of each one. If the gold leaf doesn't stick easily to the top of the marshmallow, slightly moisten the surface with a drop of water, or place the naked marshmallows one side at a time on the gold, completely encasing them in shiny magic.

Makes 30 marshmallows

Chapter 5

GROWN-UP

Who said marshmallows are just for kids? Add a little kick with cocktail ingredients such as rum, gin, and Cointreau—or melt marshmallows into vodka for a martini with a hit of sugar as well as alcohol. If you want the sweetness without the intoxication, try the liquor-free variations.

PIÑA COLADA MARSHMALLOWS

Cocktail flavorings work brilliantly in marshmallow form. Alcohol, particularly liquor, is carried well by the architecture of the sugar and egg white.

INGREDIENTS

1 cup (100g) shredded coconut
1 quantity ingredients for vanilla marshmallow mix (see page 10)
2 tablespoons (30ml) light rum
Natural yellow food coloring
2 ounces (50g) freeze-dried pineapple pieces
  (see Resources, page 144)

METHOD

Place the shredded coconut in a dry skillet over moderate heat and toast until a light golden brown color.

Make the marshmallow mix following the method on page 10. As the final step before setting the mix, add in the rum and a few drops of yellow food coloring. This will loosen the mix, but continue to whisk and the volume will return. This may take 5–10 minutes of whisking until the mixture thickens again as the gelatin sets. Stop whisking and add in the small pieces of freeze-dried pineapple. Scrape out the mix and set in a lightly oiled baking pan. When it has set, cut into cubes and toss in the toasted shredded coconut.

Makes about 20 large marshmallows

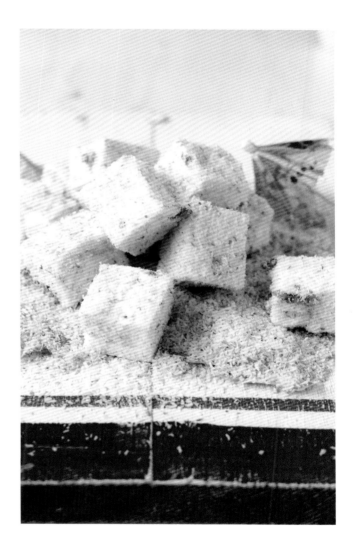

TIPS

Fresh pineapple could be used here, but it will make the final marshmallows a little wet and they won't store as well.

ALCOHOL-FREE VERSION

Omitting the rum still gives a tropical, fresh, and fruity marshmallow.

THE COSMOPOLITAN MARSHMALLOW

Obviously, you will want to try this one—Saturday night fun without the glass. Go easy. Dropping the alcohol from this recipe still gives a great-flavored marshmallow.

INGREDIENTS

1 quantity ingredients for vanilla
   marshmallow (see page 10)
Zest of 1 lime
Juice of ½ lime
1 tablespoon (15ml) Cointreau
2 tablespoons (30ml) vodka
4 teaspoons (20ml) cranberry
   juice drink
Natural red food coloring
1 quantity 50/50 coating
   (see page 10)
1 orange

METHOD

Make the marshmallow following the method on page 10. At Step 6, add the lime zest and juice. Add the alcohol and cranberry juice and a few drops of the coloring, and whisk again. It may take 5–10 minutes until the mixture thickens. Scrape out into a lightly oiled baking pan, and let set. Cut into cubes and dust with 50/50 coating mix. Cut small slices of orange zest and use to decorate the cubes.

Makes about 20 large marshmallows

ALCOHOL-FREE VERSION

Swap the Cointreau for orange cordial and omit the vodka.

SPICED RUM & RAISIN MARSHMALLOWS

Here, plump soaked golden raisins are hidden away in pillows of warming spiced rum marshmallow. They're perfect on their own or floating on the top of your favorite hot chocolate.

INGREDIENTS

⅓ cup (50g) golden raisins
6 tablespoons (100ml) dark rum
1 quantity ingredients for vanilla
   marshmallow mix
   (see page 10)
½ teaspoon ground cinnamon
¼ teaspoon ground ginger
¼ nutmeg, grated
1 quantity 50/50 coating
   (see page 10)

METHOD

Soak the golden raisins in the rum overnight, or until plump. Drain the raisins, retaining the rum. Make the marshmallow following the method on page 10. At Step 6, add 3 tablespoons of the reserved rum. Whisk the mix back to its original volume. This may take 5–10 minutes. Add the spices and raisins. Scrape into a lightly oiled baking pan to set. Once set, cut into cubes and dust with the 50/50 coating mix.

Makes about 20 large marshmallows

ALCOHOL-FREE VERSION

Soak the raisins in 6 tablespoons orange juice instead of rum.

GIN & TONIC MARSHMALLOWS

These make a great first step into the world of more unusual marshmallow flavors. They guarantee a ". . . these really taste like a gin and tonic" response. The natural botanical taste of the gin is boosted by the extra juniper.

INGREDIENTS

3 juniper berries
6 tablespoons (100ml) tonic water
1 quantity ingredients for vanilla
  marshmallow mix (see page 10)
2 tablespoons (30ml) gin
1 quantity 50/50 coating (see page 10)
About 10 thin cucumber slices

METHOD

Crush the juniper berries in a mortar and pestle and place them in a small saucepan with the tonic water. Heat gently until the tonic water has reduced down to about one-third of its original volume. Remove the juniper berries and let cool.

Make the marshmallow mix following the method on page 10. As the final step before setting, add the gin and the reduced tonic water. Whisk the mix back up to its original volume. This may take 5–10 minutes of whisking until the mixture thickens again as the gelatin sets. Then scrape it out and let set in a lightly oiled baking pan.

When it has set, cut into cubes and dust with the 50/50 coating mix. Serve each marshmallow with a thin slice of cucumber on the top.

Makes about 20 large marshmallows

ALCOHOL-FREE VERSION

Leaving the gin out of this recipe creates a delicious botanical marshmallow. An equal quantity of puréed cucumber could be added instead of the gin to heighten the fresh taste.

MARSHMALLOW VODKA

This is less of a recipe, more of a progression from sweet treat to indulgent adult drink. Start with classic vanilla marshmallows as the basis for this, but try your favorite flavored ones too.

INGREDIENTS

10 large vanilla-flavored
    marshmallows
1 cup (240ml) vodka

METHOD

Chop the marshmallows into ½-inch (1.25cm) pieces and shake in a colander to remove excess coating. Put in a Kilner or other airtight jar and pour vodka over the top. Place the lid on the jar and let infuse for 48 hours in the refrigerator. Some or all of the marshmallows may have dissolved. You'll be left with a cloudy mix. Line a colander with fine cheesecloth. Place the colander over a bowl and pour the infused vodka into it. Pour the vodka into a bottle and store in the refrigerator. Serve ice cold or use in your favorite cocktail.

BEER MARSHMALLOWS

Choose a substantial beer for this one. Frothy pale lagers won't have the depth of flavor to come alive in the marshmallow. You want something dark and earthy. Eat with salty snacks.

INGREDIENTS

5 sheets (¼ ounce/8g)
    platinum-strength leaf
    gelatin
1 ¾ cups (400ml) ale
1 teaspoon vegetable oil
1 egg white (1 ¼ ounces/35g)
1 ¼ cups (280g) superfine
    sugar
1 ½ tablespoons (25ml)
    glucose syrup
1 teaspoon vanilla extract
1 quantity 50/50 coating
    (see page 10)

METHOD

Make the marshmallow mix following the method on page 10, but with the following changes: Instead of softening the gelatin in water, bloom the sheets in 1 ¼ cups of the ale and use 4 tablespoons of the ale in place of the water for the sugar syrup. Add the remaining ale to the marshmallow mix during the final stages of whisking. This may take 5–10 minutes of whisking until the mixture thickens again as the gelatin sets. Spread into an oiled baking pan and let set. Cut into cubes and dust with 50/50 coating mix.

Makes about 20 large marshmallows

STOUT MARSHMALLOWS

Follow the recipe, but replace the ale with Irish stout and add natural black food coloring. Make a quarter batch of vanilla marshmallow mix and spread over the top. When set, cut out circles to recreate the just-served pint effect.

MARSHMALLOWTINI

Despite its frivolous sweet base, this is a really sensible and refined drink. Decorated with split vanilla beans, it's as elegant as it is delightful.

INGREDIENTS
3 tablespoons (50ml) marshmallow vodka
   (see page 70)
1 tablespoon (15ml) Grand Marnier
1 tablespoon (15ml) sugar syrup
   (see tip below)
1 vanilla bean
Ice cubes

METHOD
Mix all the ingredients other than the vanilla bean in a cocktail shaker or small pitcher. Stir gently, and then strain into a martini glass.

Split the vanilla bean down its length. Cut a small lengthwise strip and rest it in the drink.

Serves 1

TIP
Sugar syrup is made by heating equal quantities by weight of sugar and water until the sugar dissolves.

EGG NOG MARSHMALLOWS

If we're honest, no one actually enjoys egg nog, but take those flavors and combine them with a marshmallow and they become a delicious and perfect Christmas gift.

INGREDIENTS

1 quantity ingredients for vanilla marshmallow mix
    (see page 10)
2 vanilla beans
3 tablespoons (45ml) brandy
½ nutmeg, grated
Natural yellow food coloring
¼ cup (50g) candied cherries, chopped (optional)
1 quantity 50/50 coating (see page 10)

METHOD

Make the marshmallow mix following the method on page 10. Split the vanilla beans and add the seeds at Step 6. After the final whisking, add in the brandy, half the nutmeg, and a few drops of the coloring. This may take 5–10 minutes of whisking until the mixture thickens again as the gelatin sets. Fold through the cherries (if using).

Scrape out the mix and set in a lightly oiled baking pan. Once set, cut into cubes, stars, Christmas trees, or other suitable festive shapes and dust with the 50/50 coating mix. Sprinkle with the remaining nutmeg—delicious served in hot chocolate.

Makes about 30 marshmallows

ALCOHOL-FREE VERSION

This recipe can be adjusted to make an alcohol-free version by omitting the brandy and adding in the candied cherries.

Chapter 6

ADVENTUROUS

Take your taste buds on a trip around the world, or liven up a cocktail
party with marshmallow canapés. Exciting combinations include chipotle
and black cardamom, chorizo, pimentón, and lemon; try the classic potato
chip flavors of blue cheese and onion, or even salt and vinegar.

CHORIZO, PIMENTÓN & LEMON MARSHMALLOWS

Hola, Señor Marshmallow! The sweet, spicy chorizo works fabulously here. Little nuggets of savory pork goodness stud the soft, spicy marshmallow while lemon juice balances the sweetness.

INGREDIENTS

3 ounces (80g) chorizo

1 quantity ingredients for vanilla marshmallow mix (see page 10)

½ teaspoon pimentón

Zest of 1 lemon

Juice of ½ lemon

1 quantity 50/50 coating (see page 10)

METHOD

Finely chop the chorizo or blend in a food processor for about 30 seconds.

Make the marshmallow mix following the method on page 10. At the final whisking stage, add in the pimentón, lemon zest, and juice. The fat in the chorizo will cause the marshmallow to deflate a little, so add that in by folding through quickly just before scraping out the mix into a lightly oiled baking pan to set.

Once set, cut into chunks and dust with the 50/50 coating mix. Serve as a part of a mind-blowing Spanish tapas adventure.

Makes 30 marshmallows

ROASTED CHIPOTLE & BLACK CARDAMOM MARSHMALLOWS

This is more about deep smoky flavors than blow-your-head-off chili spicing. Black cardamom is a remarkable spice that works here as a powerhouse of smoked awesomeness.

INGREDIENTS

5 dried chipotle chilis
3 black cardamom pods
1 quantity ingredients for vanilla
   marshmallow mix (see page 10)
1 quantity 50/50 coating (see page 10)

METHOD

Split the chilis and remove the seeds. Press them out flat. Heat a griddle pan over high heat and place the flattened chilis on it. Cook them for 4–5 minutes until lightly browned, but be careful not to burn them.

Pour ¾ cup (180ml) cold water into a bowl. Place the chilis in the bowl and let them rehydrate for an hour or until soft. Drain the chilis but keep the water. Finely chop the chilis.

Crush the black cardamom pods and put in a small saucepan with the chili-infused water. Place over medium heat and bring to a simmer. Reduce the water to approximately one-third of its original volume. Leave the water and cardamom pods to infuse in the saucepan for 30 minutes. Remove the cardamom pods and discard.

Make the marshmallow mix following the method on page 10. Add the finely chopped chili and the chili- and cardamom-infused water at the final stage of whisking. Scrape out and let set in a lightly oiled baking pan.

Once set, cut the marshmallows and dust with the 50/50 coating mix.

Makes 30 marshmallows

MATCHA GREEN TEA MARSHMALLOWS

Matcha should be the sixth taste: salt, sweet, sour, bitter, umami, and "matchary." A grassy, puréed sensation—in the best and most wonderful sense. Matched by a green color that can't be beaten. The sweetness of the marshmallow tempers the natural tannins and bitterness of the matcha. This is one of the best ways to try matcha if you haven't. Make 'em, sunshine.

INGREDIENTS

1 tablespoon matcha green tea powder, plus extra
   for dusting
1 quantity ingredients for vanilla marshmallow mix
   (see page 10)
1 quantity 50/50 coating (see page 10)

METHOD

Put the matcha powder in a bowl and mix to a paste with 3 tablespoons water.

Make the marshmallow mix following the method on page 10, adding the matcha paste during the final whisking. Whisk until combined and a deep green color. Scrape out the marshmallow mix and set in a lightly oiled baking pan.

Once set, cut and dust with the 50/50 coating mix and matcha green tea powder.

Makes 30 large marshmallows

SPICED CARROT SOUP WITH TOASTED CORIANDER MARSHMALLOWS

Inspired by the Thanksgiving classic, sweet potatoes and marshmallows, here is a warming soup studded with fragrant, spiced marshmallows. Their sweetness heightens the natural carrot flavor and proves again that the only thing better than a marshmallow is a melted marshmallow.

INGREDIENTS

For the coriander marshmallows:
¾ cup (75g) confectioners' sugar
¾ cup (75g) cornstarch
2 teaspoons ground coriander
3 tablespoons coriander seeds
1 ½ egg whites (1 ¾ ounces/45g)
1 ¾ cups (360g) superfine sugar
2 tablespoons (35ml) glucose syrup
⅞ ounce (22g/about 13 sheets) platinum-
   strength leaf gelatin, soaked in cold water
   until soft

For the spiced carrot soup:
1 tablespoon vegetable oil
1 pound (500g) carrots, coarsely chopped
1 onion, coarsely chopped
1 celery stick, chopped
Thumb-size piece of fresh gingerroot,
   sliced (unpeeled)
2 teaspoons ground coriander
1 star anise
About 4 cups (1 liter) vegetable stock
   (made from a bouillon cube or powder
   is fine)
½ bunch of cilantro, chopped

METHOD

To make the marshmallows, line a baking pan with wax paper. Combine the confectioners' sugar, cornstarch, and ground coriander in a small bowl and lightly dust the lined baking pan with a little of the mixture.

Put the coriander seeds in a small dry skillet over moderate heat and toast until the fragrance from the seeds is released. Tip out and crush coarsely with the back of knife or mortar and pestle. Place the crushed seeds in a small pan with 5 tablespoons (75g) water and heat until it boils. Remove from the heat and infuse for 30 minutes. Strain the water into a measuring cup and add cold water to return the volume to 5 tablespoons.

Place the egg whites in the bowl of a free-standing mixer. A handheld electric mixer will also work. Mix the coriander water, superfine sugar, and glucose syrup in a medium saucepan, and heat, measuring the temperature of the syrup with a digital candy thermometer. As the temperature gets close to 250°F (120°C) start to whisk the egg white. When 250°F (120°C) is reached, pour the sugar syrup onto the egg white and continue to whisk until stiff peaks have formed.

Meanwhile, squeeze the residual water from the gelatin sheets. While the egg white is still whisking, gently melt the softened gelatin in a small saucepan over very low heat.

Pour the liquid gelatin onto the egg white and sugar syrup. Whisk back up to soft peaks.

Scrape the warm marshmallow mix into the dusted baking pan and dust the top with more of the confectioners' sugar, cornstarch, and coriander mix. Let set overnight.

Once set, chop the marshmallows into small ½-inch (1.25cm) cubes, dusting each cube again with the remaining coriander coating.

To make the carrot soup, heat the oil in a large saucepan and add the chopped vegetables and the gingerroot. Cook for 10 minutes over medium heat until softened. Add the ground coriander and star anise and cook for an additional 5 minutes.

Pour over 2 cups of the vegetable stock and bring to a boil. Simmer until the carrot is just soft. Remove the star anise and then purée with an immersion blender. Add the remaining stock until you have the consistency desired.

Pour the soup into small bowls and sprinkle with the marshmallows and chopped cilantro.

Serves 6

BLUE CHEESE & ONION MARSHMALLOWS

In the same way you'd eat cheese with sweet pickle or fruit, cheese in a marshmallow is not so strange. You need a bold and brave cheese—a punchy blue one is perfect. Not convinced? Well, they are coated in crispy onions, and as we know, everything covered in crispy onions is tasty. Fact.

INGREDIENTS

1 quantity ingredients for vanilla
   marshmallow mix (see page 10)
3 ounces (80g) blue cheese,
   finely crumbled
Vegetable oil for frying
2 onions, finely sliced

METHOD

Make the marshmallow mix following the method on page 10. Just before scraping out the mix to set, add the blue cheese. The fat in the cheese will cause the mix to collapse dramatically if you mix it too much. Add it quickly, stir it through, then quickly tip out into a lightly oiled baking pan to set.

Fill a large saucepan with vegetable oil to a depth of ½ inch (1.25cm) and place over medium heat. Add the onions in batches and fry until golden and crispy. Remove from the oil with a slotted spoon and drain on paper towels. Let cool, then chop into small pieces that are still big enough to give some crunch.

Once set, cut the marshmallows into chunks and coat in the crispy onions. These marshmallows won't keep well and are best made and eaten on the same day.

Makes 20 large marshmallows

TEMPURA MARSHMALLOWS

There's a bit of a knack to getting these to work. You'll need larger marshmallows and will have to freeze them before frying. Otherwise, the marshmallow disappears into the oil, lost forever. You'll be left with batter and a sense of emptiness.

INGREDIENTS

Your favorite marshmallows
Ice-cold sparkling mineral water
1 ½ cups (150g) tempura batter mix, or ½ cup
    (60g) cornstarch, ¾ cup (90g) all-purpose flour,
    and 2 teaspoons (5g) baking powder

Vegetable oil for deep-frying
Confectioners' sugar for dusting

METHOD

Place the marshmallows in the freezer overnight.

Add enough cold sparkling water to either the batter mix or the combined cornstarch, flour, and baking powder to create a thick batter.

Half fill a large, deep saucepan with vegetable oil and heat to 350°F (180°C).

Coat the frozen marshmallows in the batter and carefully drop the marshmallows into the hot oil. Fry for 10 seconds. Dust with confectioners' sugar and eat immediately.

Makes 15–18 marshmallows

SALT & VINEGAR MARSHMALLOWS

Stay with me on this one. If any of these more adventurous recipes need trying, it's this one. Perhaps "vinegar" is misleading since what you need here is a syrupy sweet, tangy balsamic, not what the Brits put on their fish and chips. Great as a canapé, the deep black color will intrigue and delight your guests.

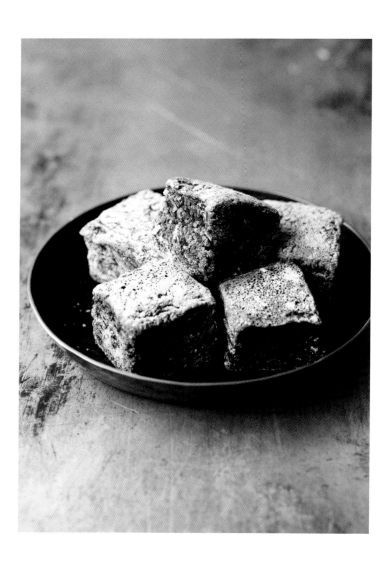

INGREDIENTS
1 quantity ingredients for vanilla marshmallow mix
  (see page 10)
1 tablespoon balsamic vinegar
¾ teaspoon fine table salt
Natural black food coloring
1 quantity 50/50 coating (see page 10)

METHOD
Make the marshmallow mix following the method on page 10, adding the vinegar, salt, and enough black food coloring to give a deep, black color during the final whisking. Check the seasoning and add more salt or vinegar if desired.

Scrape the mix into a lightly oiled baking pan to set. Once set, cut into perfect cubes and dust with the 50/50 coating mix.

Makes 30 marshmallows

TIP
Try using coarser sea salt or kosher salt as it gives a better taste, but ensure you've ground it down finely before adding it to the mix.

PORCINI MARSHMALLOWS

These achieve a powerful mushroom taste in a small mouthful. If you're feeling super extravagant, a grating of fresh truffle would raise their game still further. As tasty as these are eaten alone, they work really well melted into other dishes. A few tucked inside a baked potato or dropped into a soup would be wonderful.

INGREDIENTS

$^2/_3$ cup (30g) dried porcini mushrooms
1 quantity ingredients for vanilla
    marshmallow mix (see page 10)
1 tablespoon Worcestershire sauce
1 quantity 50/50 coating (see page 10)
1 teaspoon truffle honey (optional)

METHOD

Place ½ cup (20g) dried porcini mushrooms in a bowl and pour in just enough hot water to cover. Put the remaining porcini mushrooms in a spice grinder and blend to a fine powder, or grate with a fine Microplane grater.

When the soaked porcini are soft, finely chop them or purée them in a blender.

Make the marshmallow mix following the method on page 10, adding the finely ground dried mushrooms, chopped soaked mushrooms, and Worcestershire sauce at the final whisking stage. Scrape into a lightly oiled baking pan and let set.

Once set, chop into cubes or cut with a mushroom-shaped cookie cutter. Dust with the 50/50 coating mix. For added decadence, drizzle with a little truffle honey before serving.

Makes 20 large marshmallows

MARMITE & PRETZEL MARSHMALLOWS

Salty, savory, crunchy, and delicious. The sweetness of the marshmallow rounds off the edges of the spiky-tasting Marmite. Cut these smaller than usual since you'll want lots of coating crunch to balance the softer marshmallow. These are best consumed with a cold beer, watching sports on TV.

INGREDIENTS

1 quantity ingredients for vanilla marshmallow mix (see page 10)
1 tablespoon Marmite (see tip below)
3 ½ ounces (100g) pretzels (the small crunchy snack, not its bigger bread cousin)

METHOD

Make the marshmallow mix following the method on page 10. Just before scraping the marshmallow mix out to set, add the Marmite and whisk it in. You may want to start with ½ tablespoon then add more to taste.

Scrape out the marshmallow mix into a lightly oiled baking pan and let set.

Crush the pretzels in the bag or a bowl until you have small $\frac{1}{10}$–$\frac{1}{8}$-inch (2–3mm) pieces. Cut the marshmallow into small ¾-inch (2cm) pieces and toss in the pretzels to coat.

Makes 30 small marshmallows

TIP

Vegemite, Bovril, and other umami hot spots work just as well as Marmite. At a stretch, a bouillon cube made into a paste with a bit of water would do the trick.

Chapter 7

PARTY

Make a birthday, wedding, or just a good day at the office extra special with a marshmallow-studded cake or dessert. From frostings and sundae sauces, to Rice Krispie treats and pecan pie bark, there are plenty of options for sweet-toothed celebrations.

MARSHMALLOW POPCORN

Marshmallows and popcorn are best friends, Mrs. Marshmallow softening Mr. Popcorn's crunchiness. These are best made and eaten while still warm, served in a big bowl on the couch.

INGREDIENTS

2 tablespoons canola or vegetable oil
6 tablespoons (75g) popping corn
5 tablespoons (75g) butter
⅓ cup (75g) brown sugar
2 handfuls of vanilla marshmallows (see page 10)
¼ teaspoon sea salt

METHOD

Heat the oil in a large saucepan with a lid. Tip in the popcorn and stir briefly to coat the corn in oil. Cover and keep the pan on moderate heat until the corn starts popping. Turn the heat off and let the magic happen.

Melt the butter in a saucepan over medium heat. Add the brown sugar and the marshmallows and stir until smooth. Add the salt.

Pour the buttery, sugary marshmallow goodness over the popped corn and stir until the corn is well coated.

These will harden up over time, and if kept in an airtight container, will be good for 2–3 days.

Makes about 11 cups

MARSHMALLOW CHOCOLATE PECAN PIE BARK

This is a wonderful sweet sandwich. Perhaps it is best eaten in small pieces, but none the less, it ticks all the sweet, salty, chocolate, caramel, and marshmallow boxes. Oh, and pecans too.

INGREDIENTS

13 ounces (400g) milk chocolate
1 quantity vanilla marshmallows
   (see page 10)
1 cup (225g) superfine sugar
4 tablespoons (60g) butter
½ cup (120ml) heavy cream
¼ teaspoon salt
1 ¼ cups (150g) pecans

METHOD

Line an 8-inch (20cm) square baking pan with wax paper.

Melt the chocolate in a heatproof bowl set over a saucepan of barely simmering water (bain-marie or double-boiler). Pour half the chocolate into the lined baking pan and smooth with an offset spatula. Let set.

Melt the marshmallows in a small saucepan over low heat. Pour the melted marshmallow over the set chocolate and let that layer set.

Make the caramel sauce by heating the superfine sugar in a dry saucepan over medium heat. Watch the sugar all the time and stir it with a spoon to melt it evenly. Yes, it's okay to stir the sugar—with this method it won't crystallize if stirred. When the sugar has melted to a light brown caramel, add the butter and cream. At this point the caramel will spit. Be careful.

Continue to stir over medium heat, and the crystallized sugar will melt away. Once all the sugar has melted and the sauce is smooth, cook for an additional 2 minutes. Add the salt and let cool.

Sprinkle the pecans over the marshmallow and pour the caramel over the top. Place in the refrigerator until the caramel is firm. Reheat the remaining chocolate and pour over the top of the caramel and nuts. Let set completely. Then remove from the tray and break into pieces.

Makes 30 marshmallows

MARSHMALLOW & PISTACHIO CHOCOLATE FUDGE

Bejeweled with pistachios and marshmallows, this fudge would make a great gift gathered into clear plastic gift bags and tied with ribbon. This is a fudgy fudge, not a grainy fudge—the glucose and the chocolate see to that.

INGREDIENTS

4 ½ ounces (140g) milk chocolate
2 cups (480ml) heavy cream
2 ½ cups (500g) superfine sugar
4 ½ tablespoons (80ml) glucose syrup
1 ¼ cups (150g) shelled pistachios
2 handfuls of vanilla marshmallows (see page 10),
   chopped into ½-inch (2.5cm) cubes

METHOD

Lightly grease an 8-inch (20cm) square pan.

Melt the chocolate in a heatproof bowl over a saucepan of barely simmering water (bain-marie or double-boiler). Keep the chocolate warm and molten.

Put the cream, sugar, and glucose syrup in a saucepan and stir together over medium heat. Stir continuously and measure the temperature. When the mixture reaches 244°F (118°C), remove from the heat and stir in the melted chocolate. Then add the nuts and pour into the greased pan. Let the fudge cool a little, then sprinkle with the marshmallow cubes. You need it at a temperature that doesn't melt the marshmallows too much but does let them stick to the top of the fudge.

Let set fully, then cut into squares and serve.

Makes 30 pieces

MARSHMALLOW SKEWERS

The fun here is the construction. Perfect as a children's birthday party activity, these might be best scheduled for the end of the party so the chocolate- and sprinkle-covered, sticky-fingered guests can be propelled quickly into the arms of delighted parents.

INGREDIENTS

13 ounces (400g) semisweet chocolate
1 quantity vanilla marshmallows
    (see page 10)

Wooden skewers

For the coatings:
Finely chopped hazelnuts
Chocolate sprinkles
Popping candy
Ice-cream sprinkles

Water icing (confectioners' sugar and water
    mixed to a pipeable paste)

METHOD

Melt the chocolate in a heatproof bowl set over a saucepan of barely simmering water (bain-marie or double-boiler) and stir gently until melted.

Place the bowl of melted chocolate in the middle of a well-protected table. Slide the marshmallows onto wooden skewers, then dunk into the chocolate.

Place the coatings in small bowls and sprinkle over the marshmallows. Let the skewers set. They can be held up to dry and harden by pushing the ends of the skewers into a Styrofoam box or a melon cut in half and placed cut side down on a dish.

Put the water icing into a pastry bag with a small ($\frac{1}{16}$-inch/1mm) round tip. Decorate and drizzle the coated marshmallows.

Makes 6–8 skewers

STUFFED BEURRE NOISETTE MARSHMALLOW RICE KRISPIE CAKES

Hold onto your hats, this is a Rice Krispie treat that is an 11 out of 10 on the flavor scale— proving again the amazing effect beurre noisette has on cakes and the versatility of marshmallow as an ingredient.

INGREDIENTS

- 1 ½ quantities ingredients for vanilla marshmallow mix (see page 10)
- 1 ½ teaspoons vanilla extract
- 3 ½ tablespoons (50g) butter
- ¼ teaspoon salt
- 7 ½ cups (200g) Rice Krispies

METHOD

Lightly grease two 12 x 8-inch (30 x 20cm) baking pans.

Make the marshmallow mix following the method on page 10, and flavor with the vanilla at step 6. During the final whisking stage, start to melt the butter in a large saucepan. Continue to heat until the butter foams and starts to turn a light brown color. Remove the saucepan from the heat.

Remove two-thirds of the marshmallow mix from the mixer bowl and stir into the brown butter. Add the salt and stir the mix until smooth. Add in the Rice Krispies and stir until well combined. Put half of the Krispie mix into each pan. Place in the refrigerator to set firm. Keep the remaining marshmallow mix to one side. It will set but that's okay.

Once the mix has set, remove one of the sheets of Rice Krispie cake from the baking pan and set aside. Warm up the remaining one-third marshmallow mix by placing the bowl over a saucepan of simmering water and stirring until loose and smooth. Tip this onto the Rice Krispie cake in its pan and press the other cake on top.

Let the whole thing set again and then cut into squares. Scrumptious.

Makes 16 squares

MARSHMALLOW RICE KRISPIE CAKES

This is the never-fails-to-please children's party classic. A classic because, like all the best children's party food, it's most enjoyed by adults. Make more than you need. They'll get eaten.

INGREDIENTS
3 ½ tablespoons (50g) butter
1 quantity vanilla marshmallows
   (see page 10)
7 ½ cups (200g) Rice Krispies

METHOD
Lightly grease a 12 x 8-inch (30 x 20cm) baking pan.

Melt the butter in a large saucepan over medium heat. Once melted, add the marshmallows and stir until dissolved and you have a smooth sauce. Remove the saucepan from the heat.

Tip the Rice Krispies into the butter and marshmallow mix and stir well. Spoon the mix into the prepared baking pan. Press it down with the back of a large spoon until well compacted. Yes, it will be sticky, but lick your fingers.

Let cool until hard then remove from the pan and cut into squares.

Makes 16 squares

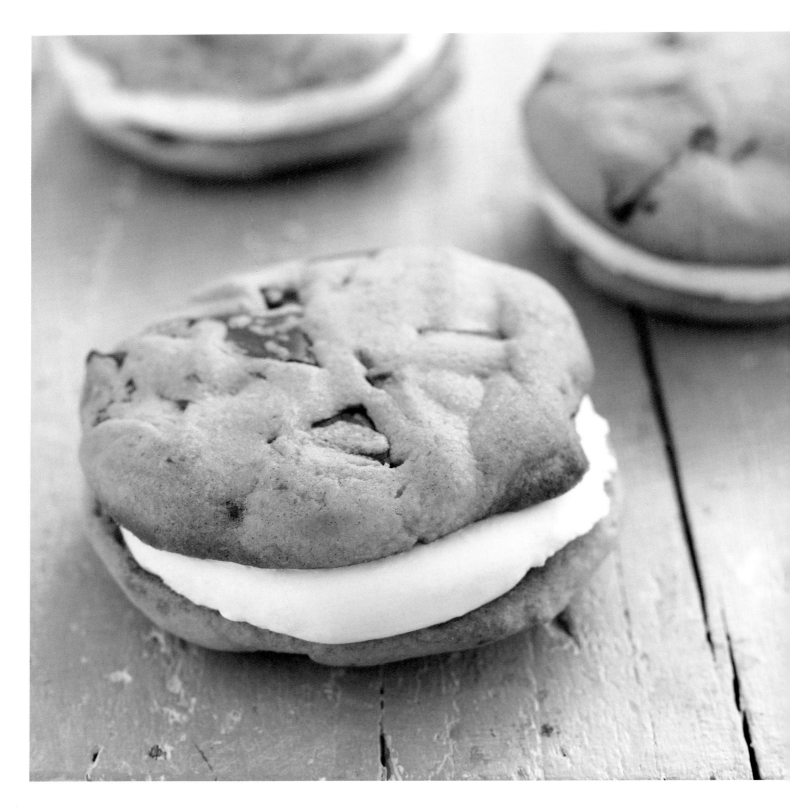

MARSHMALLOW CHOCOLATE CHIP COOKIE SANDWICHES

Ooh-la-la, these are tasty. Using the same principle as ice-cream sandwiches, here dense and chewy chocolate chip cookies are sandwiched together with soft marshmallow. The advantage is that they won't melt so easily and can be kept in lunch boxes and bags for covert eating. Try constructing them while the cookies are still warm. Eaten just after filling, they are scrumptious.

INGREDIENTS

¼ cup (50g) superfine sugar
¼ cup (50g) light brown sugar
9 tablespoons (125g) butter
 (at room temperature)
1 egg
½ teaspoon vanilla extract
½ teaspoon salt
1 cup (225g) self-rising flour
6 ounces (180g) milk chocolate
½ quantity ingredients for vanilla
 marshmallow mix (see page 10)

METHOD

Preheat the oven to 400°F (200°C). Line two cookie sheets with parchment paper.

Cream together the sugars and the butter in a large bowl until pale and fluffy. Add the egg and beat until smooth. Add the vanilla and salt, then fold in the flour. Chop the chocolate into coarse chunks no bigger than ½ inch (1.25cm).

Using a medium ice-cream scoop, make round mounds of dough and evenly space them on the cookie sheets. Flatten them a little with your hand. Bake in the oven for 8–10 minutes until the edges are starting to brown but the centers are still soft.

While the cookies bake, make the vanilla marshmallow mix following the method on page 10. When the cookies are done, spoon or pipe the marshmallow onto the flat base of one cookie. Fill generously, there's no harm in the marshmallow oozing out a little. Place another cookie on top. EAT!

Makes 7–8 cookie sandwiches

SALTED CARAMEL MARSHMALLOW TEACAKES

Here is a cheeky little twist on the British teatime classic. Sometimes it's hard not to add salted caramel to everything, but here that salt helps to cut through what's otherwise a rather sweet cake. Making these is a bit tricky, but one bite and you'll know it was all worthwhile.

For the cookies:
2 tablespoons (30g) butter
2 tablespoons (30g) superfine sugar
Pinch of salt
¾ cup (100g) all-purpose flour
1 tablespoon milk

For the salted caramel sauce:
¼ cup (50g) superfine sugar
6 tablespoons (100ml) heavy cream
2 tablespoons (30g) butter
½ teaspoon sea salt

13 ounces (400g) semisweet chocolate
1 quantity vanilla marshmallow frosting
  (see page 106)
Silicone demisphere mold with a sphere
  diameter of 2 ¾ inches (7cm)
  (see Resources, page 144)

METHOD

Line a cookie sheet with parchment paper.

To make the cookies, cream the butter and sugar together in a bowl. Add the salt and flour and mix together with your hands or in a free-standing mixer. Add the milk and work the dough into a smooth ball. Cover with plastic wrap and chill in the refrigerator for an hour.

Roll out the dough on a floured work surface to about ⅛ inch (3mm) thick. Cut out six 2 ¾-inch (7cm) round cookies and place on the lined cookie sheet. Refrigerate the cookies again for 1 hour.

Preheat the oven to 325°F (160°C). Bake the cookies from chilled for 9–10 minutes until firm and an even brown color. Let cool.

The chocolate coating is ideally made from tempered chocolate. The detail of how to do that is beyond the scope of this book, but there are excellent videos on the technique online. If not tempering, melt the chocolate in a heatproof bowl placed over a saucepan of barely simmering water (bain-marie or double-boiler). Let the chocolate cool and thicken slightly and then coat the insides of the demispheres with an even layer of the chocolate. This won't require all the chocolate. Reserve the remaining chocolate and let the chocolate-coated molds cool.

To make the salted caramel sauce, place the superfine sugar in a medium saucepan and heat gently over moderate heat. Move the sugar around the saucepan by gently tipping it. It's okay to stir the caramel with this method if it's melting unevenly. As soon as it has turned a light brown color, pour in the cream and butter. This creates lots of steam and fussing in the saucepan. The caramel will seize and look awful, but keep stirring and the sugar will melt back into the cream. Once it has all melted and is smooth, cook on moderate heat for 2 minutes or until thickened slightly. Add the salt and let cool.

Make the marshmallow frosting following the method on page 106.

To construct the teacakes, pipe or spoon a teaspoon of salted caramel sauce into the bottom of each chocolate-coated mold. Then pipe in the marshmallow frosting to just below the surface.

Warm the reserved chocolate. Dunk one side of a cookie in the chocolate then press that side onto the marshmallow. Use any remaining chocolate to seal and neaten the join between cookie, marshmallow, and chocolate dome. Repeat for each of the cakes. Let the complete teacakes set.

Carefully demold and admire your hard work.

Makes 6

GRAND MARSHMALLOW WEDDING CAKE

You're going to need a lot of marshmallows, but the effect is impressive and far more fun and interesting than a sugar paste-covered fruit cake. The marshmallows can be made over a week or two and stored in airtight containers until construction.

INGREDIENTS

Styrofoam tower
Food-safe tissue paper
Lots of toothpicks
Lots of marshmallows (see tip below)

METHOD

Cover the tower with the food-safe tissue of your choice. Wrap it tightly and fix with small pieces of adhesive tape.

Starting at the bottom, push toothpicks into the tower then slide the marshmallows on. If you use alternating colors of marshmallows you'll slowly build a spiral effect as the marshmallows build.

The tower can be positioned on top of a more traditional cake if you want something to cut into. Construct the tower and place on a thin cake board. Dowel the cake so the tower's weight is supported, and simply rest on top.

Decoration: These towers cry out for over-the-top decoration—think rose petals, candy canes, sugarpaste flowers, spirals of ribbon, and sparklers in the top. A wedding cake for the young at heart.

TIP

Styrofoam towers come in many sizes. As a guide, if using plain round cut marshmallows 1 ¼ inches (3cm) in diameter:

- 8 inches (20cm) high, 3 ½-inch (9cm) diameter base —40 marshmallows
- 12 inches (30.5cm) high, 4 ¼-inch (11.5cm) diameter base —90 marshmallows
- 22 inches (56cm) high, 6 ¾-inch (17cm) diameter base —170 marshmallows

The exact numbers you'll need will vary significantly depending on how closely you place the marshmallows.

BEURRE NOISETTE MARSHMALLOW SAUCE

Poured over your favorite baked treats such as brownies and waffles, or drizzled over ice cream, this sauce is difficult to beat. The beurre noisette (brown butter) adds a complex nutty taste. It also brings a little French refinement.

INGREDIENTS

3 ½ tablespoons (50g) butter
¼ cup (50g) superfine sugar
1 ⅛ cups (275ml) heavy cream
2 handfuls of vanilla marshmallows
   (see page 10)

METHOD

Warm the butter in a small saucepan over medium heat. Let it melt and then froth. Watch it carefully. The butter will continue to froth, and the foam will begin to turn a light brown color. This is the point when the milk solids in the butter begin to caramelize. The butter will begin to smell nutty. At this point, remove from the heat and let cool a little.

The butter can be used in the sauce right away, but for a cleaner appearance, the milk solids at the bottom of the pan can be filtered out. Place a paper towel in a fine strainer and pass the butter through.

Return the filtered butter to the pan. Add the superfine sugar to the warm butter and stir until dissolved. Add the cream and bring to a simmer. Toss in the marshmallows and stir until smooth and unctuous.

TIP

Obviously, different marshmallow flavors will give different flavored sauces. Try salted caramel sauce with fresh waffles or triple chocolate marshmallows on vanilla ice cream. Boom!

SHERBET DIPPING MARSHMALLOWS

Sherbet is the best, right? At school we made sherbet fingers. It involved licking your finger and dipping it in sherbet. Licking your finger again, but leaving some sherbet . . . and repeat. You ended up with a sherbet-cocooned finger. Amazing. If that hasn't put you off for life—try these.

INGREDIENTS

1 quantity ingredients for vanilla
    marshmallow mix (see page 10)
½ cup (50g) confectioners' sugar
1 teaspoon citric acid
    (see Resources, page 144)
1 teaspoon baking soda
Freeze-dried fruit powders—try raspberry,
    strawberry, or blueberry
    (see Resources, page 144)

METHOD

Make the marshmallow mix following the method on page 10, and leave undusted. Cut out cubes.

In a small food processor or spice grinder, mix together the confectioners' sugar, citric acid, and baking soda. This should give a fine dusty powder. Add 1 tablespoon fruit powder to the sherbet mix.

Dip the marshmallow into sherbet to coat half of it, and eat.

Makes 30

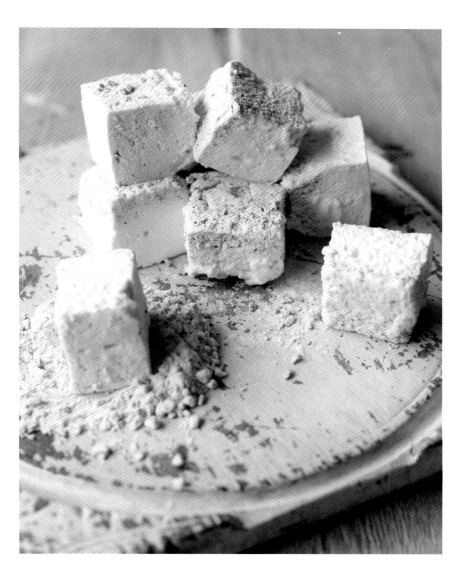

CHOCOLATE ORANGE MELTED MARSHMALLOW FONDUE

Melting marshmallows into a warm chocolate sauce adds flavor but also a great stringy texture. To balance the rich sauce, you'll need to dunk in fresh juicy fruit . . . or, when no one's watching, use more marshmallows. The addition of orange zest also helps to lighten the sauce, but feel free to leave it out if that's not your thing.

INGREDIENTS

13 ounces (400g) milk chocolate
1 cup (240ml) heavy cream
4 tablespoons (60ml) milk
Zest of 1 large orange, finely grated
Fresh fruit to dip in—banana, strawberries, and grapes
2 handfuls of vanilla marshmallows (see page 10)

METHOD

Break the chocolate into small pieces and put in a small saucepan with the cream and milk. Place over low heat. Stir gently until the chocolate has melted. Add the orange zest.

When ready to serve, prepare the fruit: slice bananas and cut any large strawberries in half. Warm the chocolate sauce. Seat your guests.

Toss the marshmallows into the melted chocolate sauce and stir until they begin to melt. Transfer the mix to a fondue pot before the marshmallows completely dissolve. Start dunking.

Serves 6

TOASTED MARSHMALLOW CLOTTED CREAM ICE CREAM

The smoky, burned sugar taste of toasted marshmallow mixed through soft vanilla ice cream is a joy. Don't be afraid to really toast the marshmallows. Those crunchy brown sugar nuggets are ice cream gold. Combined with clotted cream, this is an extraordinary dessert.

INGREDIENTS

2 large eggs
2 egg yolks
¾ cup (150g) superfine sugar
1 cup (240ml) heavy cream
1 cup (240ml) milk
8 ounces (225g) clotted cream
(if unavailable use 1 cup/240ml heavy
cream instead)
2 handfuls of vanilla marshmallows
(see page 10)

METHOD

Whisk together the whole eggs, egg yolks, and sugar in a bowl. Put the heavy cream and milk in a saucepan and warm to just boiling.

Pour approximately one-quarter of the hot cream and milk onto the eggs and sugar and stir until smooth. Tip this mix back into the remaining cream and milk, and warm gently, stirring until thickened. Remove from the heat and let cool in a clean bowl. Refrigerate until cold, then whisk through the clotted cream.

Line the marshmallows up on a cookie sheet. They can be either placed underneath a very hot broiler and toasted, or flamed with a kitchen torch. The marshmallows will puff up, some may catch fire. That's all good. When they are all nicely charred, scrape them up and blend them in a food processor.

Add the toasted marshmallow paste into the chilled ice-cream mix, pour into an ice-cream machine, and churn until soft.

Serves 8

TIP

If you prefer, the ice cream can be churned first and the charred marshmallow pieces added toward the end to create small pockets of burned marshmallow excitement.

S'MORES ICE-CREAM SUNDAES

On a hot summer's day, what better than a dessert to remind you of the colder dark times around the corner? Soak up the sun and be thankful. These work particularly well if you use the toasted marshmallow clotted cream ice cream on page 103.

INGREDIENTS

For the chocolate sauce:
3 ½ ounces (100g) semisweet chocolate
¼ cup (30g) confectioners' sugar
⅓ cup (100g) light corn syrup
⅓ cup (80ml) heavy cream
Pinch of salt

4 graham crackers
2 cups (4 scoops) vanilla or toasted
   marshmallow clotted cream ice cream
   (see page 103)
½ quantity vanilla marshmallow frosting
   (see page 106)
1 handful of vanilla marshmallows
   (see page 10)

METHOD

Make the chocolate sauce by breaking the chocolate in pieces and melting it in a heatproof bowl set over a saucepan of barely simmering water (bain-marie or double-boiler). Once melted, stir in the sugar, syrup, cream, and salt.

Crumble two crackers into the bases of four sundae glasses or bowls. Scoop in half the ice cream on top of the crumbs. Pipe or spoon in half the marshmallow frosting, then drizzle with a little of the chocolate sauce. Tumble in some marshmallows. Add the remaining ice cream and marshmallow frosting. Drizzle with more chocolate sauce, and then add more cracker crumbs on the top.

Position the remaining marshmallows on top of each sundae and use a kitchen torch to scorch the marshmallow to perfection. Eat with big spoons and gusto.

Serves 4

VANILLA MARSHMALLOW FROSTING

This voluminous creamy delight isn't a marshmallow in the "set with gelatin" sense but certainly recreates that fluffy effect. It's where marshmallow meets meringue. The egg whites are cooked with the sugar in a bain-marie or double-boiler and then stabilized with the cream of tartar.

INGREDIENTS

6 medium egg whites (7 ounces/210g)
1 ¾ cups (360g) superfine sugar
¼ teaspoon cream of tartar
Seeds from 2 vanilla beans or 1 teaspoon
    vanilla extract

METHOD

Place the egg whites and superfine sugar in a heatproof bowl. Ideally, use the bowl of your free-standing mixer as this will mean you don't have to transfer it for the final whisking. Rest the bowl over a saucepan of simmering water. Ensure the bottom of the bowl doesn't touch the water.

Whisk the egg whites and sugar continuously while measuring the temperature with a digital candy thermometer. You need to reach a temperature of 143°F (61°C), which is the point at which the egg white is cooked. Remove from the pan and place in the free-standing mixer, or begin to whisk with an electric handmixer.

Whisk to stiff peaks, then stir in the cream of tartar and the vanilla. Use immediately.

Makes enough to fill and frost an 8-inch (20cm) diameter cake

TIP

This meringue/marshmallow recipe works really well baked in a low oven. It gives a particularly dense and close structure that can be used to make meringue shapes and decorations. This should be your go-to recipe for meringue mushrooms and snowmen.

MARSHMALLOW BUTTERCREAM FROSTING

This is a simple way of incorporating new flavors into your favorite cakes. It takes a simple buttercream recipe and blends that with melted marshmallow. Change the marshmallow; change the flavor. It works particularly well if you add unmelted marshmallows as a decoration.

INGREDIENTS

½ cup (120g) sweet butter
2 cups (240g) confectioners' sugar, sifted
1 tablespoon milk
2 handfuls marshmallows

METHOD

Beat the butter in a bowl until soft, then slowly add the sifted confectioners' sugar. If you prefer, this can all be done in a food processor. Beat until smooth and then add the milk to loosen the mix a little.

Melt the marshmallows in a saucepan over low heat. You will need to stir them all the time. Almost certainly, some of the marshmallow will stick to the base of the saucepan. Once the marshmallow has melted, let it cool slightly. If it's too hot it will melt the butter and you'll have a sauce, not a frosting. When slightly cooled, beat the melted marshmallow into the buttercream and use to decorate sponge and cupcakes.

TIP

This will be the only time we mention it, but there is something called marshmallow fluff. It comes in a jar. Obviously, having read this book and made every recipe, you'll have come to appreciate that the world no longer requires this . . . fluff. However, if you used some here, instead of melting marshmallows, it would probably be acceptable and save a little time.

TOASTED MARSHMALLOW MILKSHAKES

These milky treats work well as a straightforward children's favorite, or with the addition of a little coffee liqueur, can be transformed into a much more exciting adult drink.

INGREDIENTS

5 large vanilla marshmallows (see page 10)
1 cup (2 scoops) vanilla ice cream
½ cup (120ml) milk

METHOD

Scorch four of the marshmallows with a kitchen torch until charred, puffed, and browned all over. Alternatively, place them under a hot broiler for a few seconds until ready.

Put the ice cream and milk into a blender and scrape in the charred marshmallows. Blend until smooth. Pour into a tall glass and float the last marshmallow on the top. Scorch that marshmallow with the kitchen torch as it floats.

Serve with a stripy straw.

Serves 1

TIP

For an adult version, add 1 ½ tablespoons coffee liqueur (Kahlúa) before blending.

Chapter 8

CAKES & DESSERTS

We all know how good marshmallows taste in rocky road and s'mores, but they also add an extra dimension to many more classic cake and dessert recipes. Try them instead of the meringue on a lemon meringue pie, in brownies and blondies, and to frost a carrot cake.

GROWN-UP ROCKY ROAD

Don't underestimate this classic. Think of the sweet chocolate and butter foundation as a canvas to be embroidered with delicious and exotic delights. Obviously, the marshmallows need pride of place, but use your imagination and add your candied and nutty favorites.

INGREDIENTS

5 ounces (150g) semisweet chocolate
7 ounces (200g) milk chocolate
6 tablespoons (80g) butter
1 tablespoon light corn syrup
½ cup (50g) shelled pistachios
1 handful of vanilla marshmallows (see page 10), chopped into ½-inch (1.25cm) cubes
4 pieces of candied ginger, coarsely chopped
4 tablespoons mixed candied peel
3 ounces (80g) cookies, crushed into small pieces—try gingersnaps or graham crackers

METHOD

Line a 6-inch (15cm) square pan with overlapping sheets of plastic wrap.

Melt the chocolates, butter, and syrup together in a bowl placed over a saucepan of simmering water. Make sure the base of the bowl isn't touching the water.

When melted, remove from the heat and stir in the remaining ingredients. Push down into the lined pan and let set in the refrigerator.

When set, cut into squares.

Makes 30

TIPS

The appearance of this rocky road can be heightened by setting it in different molds. Using a yule log pan, as in the marshmallow bûche cake recipe on page 140, gives a more refined look. It is only rocky road, but a wisp or two of gold leaf decorating a slice wouldn't go amiss.

PBJ CARAMEL MARSHMALLOW BARS

This recipe is a distillation of guilty food pleasures and all the better for it. Freeze-dried fruit is available in supermarkets now and a great way of packing fruit flavor into cakes and cookies.

INGREDIENTS

¾ cup (150g) smooth peanut butter
7 tablespoons (100g) butter
⅔ cup (100g) shelled peanuts
2 handfuls of vanilla marshmallows
  (see page 10), chopped into
  ½-inch (1.25cm) cubes
¼ ounce (10g) freeze-dried
  raspberries
¼ cup (50g) superfine sugar
6 tablespoons (100ml) heavy cream
¼ teaspoon salt

METHOD

Melt the peanut butter and butter in a saucepan over low heat. Stir through the peanuts, marshmallows, and raspberries. Press into the bottom of an 8-inch (20cm) square pan. Place the sugar in a small saucepan over medium heat. Stir with a spoon to help it melt and caramelize evenly. When it is a light brown color, tip in the cream. It will spit, but ignore it and keep stirring. Stir continuously until you have a smooth, deep brown sauce. Add the salt. Drizzle over the peanut and marshmallow mix. Refrigerate the mix in the pan until firm. Cut into small squares.

Makes 30

CHOCOLATE MARSHMALLOW NUT BLONDIES

Using white chocolate creates a creamy rich vanilla blondie. The marshmallows act as a frosting. The macadamia nuts help balance the texture with some additional crunch.

INGREDIENTS

4 ounces (125g) white chocolate
9 tablespoons (125g) butter
2 eggs, beaten
1 cup (225g) unrefined
  superfine sugar
¾ cup (100g) all-purpose flour
½ teaspoon baking powder
¾ cup (100g) macadamia nuts
2 handfuls of vanilla marshmallows,
  sliced (see page 10)

METHOD

Preheat the oven to 350°F (180°C). Line an 8-inch (20cm) square baking pan with parchment paper.

Melt the chocolate and butter in a heatproof bowl over a saucepan of simmering water (bain-marie or double-boiler). Mix the eggs and sugar in a bowl—then mix through the chocolate and butter. Fold in the flour and baking powder. Add the nuts. Scrape into the prepared pan and level. Layer the sliced marshmallows over the blondie mix. Bake for 20 minutes. The mix should be set around the edge but still a little soft in the middle. Bake for a little longer if needed. Cool—then refrigerate in the pan overnight. Cut into squares.

Makes 30

MARSHMALLOW-CRUSTED BLUEBERRY MUFFINS

These are best eaten warm so the molten marshmallow and hot blueberries can work their magic on your palate. The toasted vanilla top adds textural contrast to the warm muffin underneath.

INGREDIENTS

1 ½ cups (200g) all-purpose flour
⅓ cup (60g) superfine sugar
Pinch of salt
½ teaspoon baking soda
2 teaspoons baking powder
5 tablespoons (70g) sweet butter
¾ cup (180ml) buttermilk
1 egg
1 ¼ cups (150g) blueberries
24 large vanilla marshmallows (see page 10)

METHOD

Preheat the oven to 400°F (200°C). Combine the flour, sugar, salt, baking soda, and baking powder in a bowl. Melt the butter, then combine in another bowl with the buttermilk. Beat the egg and add to the buttermilk mixture.

Add the wet ingredients into the flour mixture, and mix briefly. Don't overwork the batter. Stir in the blueberries. Spoon the batter into muffin cups. Push one whole marshmallow into the center of each. Slice the remaining marshmallows and lay them over the top of the mix. Bake in the oven for 15–18 minutes or until well risen and golden.

Makes 12

CHOCOLATE MARSHMALLOW BROWNIES

The trick to these brownies is baking them properly. As with all brownies, it is better to underbake than overbake. Allowing the brownies to cool and then chilling them overnight creates a dense, fudgy texture.

INGREDIENTS

4 ounces (125g) semisweet chocolate
9 tablespoons (125g) butter
2 eggs, beaten
1 cup (225g) brown sugar
¾ cup (100g) all-purpose flour
¼ cup (25g) unsweetened cocoa
½ teaspoon baking powder
2 handfuls of vanilla marshmallows
   (see page 10)

METHOD

Preheat the oven to 350°F (180°C). Line an 8-inch (20cm) square baking pan with parchment paper.

Melt the chocolate and butter together in a heatproof bowl over a saucepan of simmering water (bain-marie or double-boiler).

Mix together the eggs and sugar in a bowl then mix through the melted chocolate and butter. Fold in the flour, cocoa, and baking powder.

Keep the marshmallows in large, approximately 1-inch (2.5cm), pieces and fold through the brownie mix.

Scrape the mix into the prepared baking pan and level. Bake in the oven for 20 minutes. Check them. The mix should be set around the edge but it's best if still a little soft in the middle. Bake for a little longer if needed. Remove from the oven and cool—then refrigerate the brownies in the pan overnight. Cut into squares.

Makes 30

WHITE CHOCOLATE & CARDAMOM MARSHMALLOW MOUSSE

Cardamom and white chocolate work wonderfully together. It scents the chocolate with intriguing lemony tones, making a grown-up and complex dessert that's brilliantly quick and simple to make. The marshmallow acts as an egg white substitute that both sweetens and lightens the mousse.

INGREDIENTS
8 plump cardamom pods
3 tablespoons (50ml) milk
8 ounces (225g) white chocolate
2 handfuls of vanilla marshmallows
   (see page 10), chopped into
   ½-inch (1.25cm) cubes
4 tablespoons (60g) butter
1 ¼ cups (300ml) heavy cream

METHOD
Crush the cardamom pods to release the seeds and place them in a small saucepan with the milk. Gently warm the milk until it just starts to boil. Remove from the heat and let infuse for 1 hour. Strain the milk through a fine strainer and set aside.

Chop the chocolate and place with the marshmallows and butter in a heatproof bowl over a saucepan of simmering water (bain-marie or double-boiler). When they have melted, add the infused milk. Stir until smooth, and then let cool a little.

Whisk the cream to soft peaks, then fold in the white chocolate mix. Spoon into individual glasses or one large serving bowl. Refrigerate.

Serves 6

CHOCOLATE CHIP MARSHMALLOW MACARONS

I couldn't resist this recipe. It's a mix of highfalutin' French patisserie and common cookie sandwich. It succeeds or fails on how well the components contrast. Macaron shells require patience to get right, but once perfected, you'll have an impressive skill up your sleeve.

INGREDIENTS

1 ¾ cups (200g) almond meal
1 ⅔ cups (200g) confectioners' sugar
4–5 (5 ounces/150g) egg whites
1 cup (200g) superfine sugar
Unsweetened cocoa for dusting
½ quantity ingredients for vanilla
   marshmallow mix (see page 10)
⅔ cup (100g) semisweet
   chocolate chips

METHOD

Preheat the oven to 300°F (150°C). Line a cookie sheet with silicone parchment paper. Combine the almonds, confectioners' sugar, and half the egg white in a bowl. Mix well until you have a thick paste.

Mix the superfine sugar and 3 tablespoons (50ml) water in a saucepan. Stir until the consistency of wet sand. Put the remaining egg white in the bowl of a free-standing mixer or use a bowl and a handheld electric mixer. Heat the sugar and water to create a syrup. While the sugar syrup is heating, whisk the egg white to soft peaks. When the sugar syrup reaches 243°F (117°C) on a digital candy thermometer, pour onto the egg white and whisk until it forms stiff peaks.

Combine this meringue with the almond meal and confectioners' sugar paste. Beat together slowly for 30 seconds then scrape down the sides of the bowl with a spatula and beat again for 30 seconds. The mix should flow smoothly, and when dropped back into the bowl, it should spread and form a flat even surface.

Transfer to a pastry bag fitted with a ½-inch (1.25cm) plain round tip. Pipe twenty 3 ¼-inch (8.25cm) circles onto the lined cookie sheet. Dust lightly with cocoa. Place in the oven and turn it off. After 10 minutes, turn the heat to 300°F (150°C) and bake for 10 minutes. Remove from the oven and let cool on the sheet. Peel the shells off the parchment paper and pair up equal-size shells.

Make the vanilla marshmallow mix following the method on page 10. Pipe onto half the macaron shells and sprinkle with chocolate chips. Sandwich a second macaron shell on top and let set.

Makes 10

BAKED S'MORES

Avoid those marshmallows falling-off-the-fork-into-the-bonfire disasters or molten-chocolate-running-down-your-arm catastrophes. Let's face it, making s'mores can be a traumatic business—and perhaps only 1 in 10 works perfectly. Your problems are solved: make these and relax.

INGREDIENTS

½ cup (100g) light brown sugar
9 tablespoons (125g) butter, room temperature
½ teaspoon vanilla extract
1 egg
½ teaspoon salt
1 ¾ cups (225g) self-rising flour
7 ounces (200g) milk chocolate cut into ¾–1 ¼-inch
   (2–3cm) chunks
½ quantity vanilla marshmallows (see page 10)

METHOD

Preheat the oven to 350°F (180°C).

Cream together the sugar and butter in a bowl or a free-standing mixer. Add the vanilla extract, egg, and salt. Mix until well combined. Sift in the flour and mix together to form a cookie dough. Push evenly into the bottom of an 8-inch (20cm) square pan and bake for 15 minutes or until golden brown.

Distribute the chocolate over the crust and return to the oven for 2 minutes. Cover with the marshmallows, return to the oven for 10 minutes, and bake to an even brown color. Cool for 15 minutes then cut into squares and serve.

Makes 30

TIP

The black cardamom and chipotle chili marshmallows (see page 76) work well here—recreating a smoky bonfire taste.

CARROT & ORANGE CAKE WITH MARSHMALLOW CREAM CHEESE FROSTING

Carrot cakes are one of those treats that are conjured up in minutes. Ohh, I fancy a piece of carrot cake, ahh I'm eating a piece of carrot cake. That was easy. Every kitchen pantry should have a box marked "EMERGENCY CAKE KIT" stocked with the ingredients below. Construct in case of emotional catastrophe, injured pets, or snowstorms.

INGREDIENTS

1 cup (200g) light brown sugar
¾ cup (180ml) vegetable oil
4 eggs
1 ½ cups (200g) self-rising flour
1 teaspoon baking soda
1 teaspoon ground cinnamon
½ teaspoon ground ginger
½ teaspoon grated nutmeg
¼ teaspoon ground cloves
Zest of 1 orange
1 cup (160g) shredded carrots
¾ cup (120g) golden raisins

For the frosting:
¾ cup (200g) cream cheese
½ quantity vanilla marshmallow frosting
   (see page 106)
Ground cinnamon, for dusting

METHOD

Preheat the oven to 350°F (180°C). Grease an 8-inch (20cm) cake pan and line with parchment paper.

Mix together the sugar, oil, and eggs in a bowl and beat until smooth.

Mix the flour, baking soda, spices, and orange zest in another bowl. Don't bother sifting the flour, it makes no difference. Add the egg mixture to the flour mix and stir to combine. Add in the shredded carrot and golden raisins.

Pour the batter into the prepared cake pan and bake for 35–40 minutes. It's cooked if it springs back when pressed and a toothpick inserted into the center comes out clean. Let it cool in the pan to firm up a bit, then turn it out onto a wire rack. Let cool completely.

To make the frosting, beat the cream cheese in a bowl until smooth, then dollop in the marshmallow frosting. Mix to combine, and then smother the cooled cake in it. Dust with extra cinnamon.

Serves 8–10

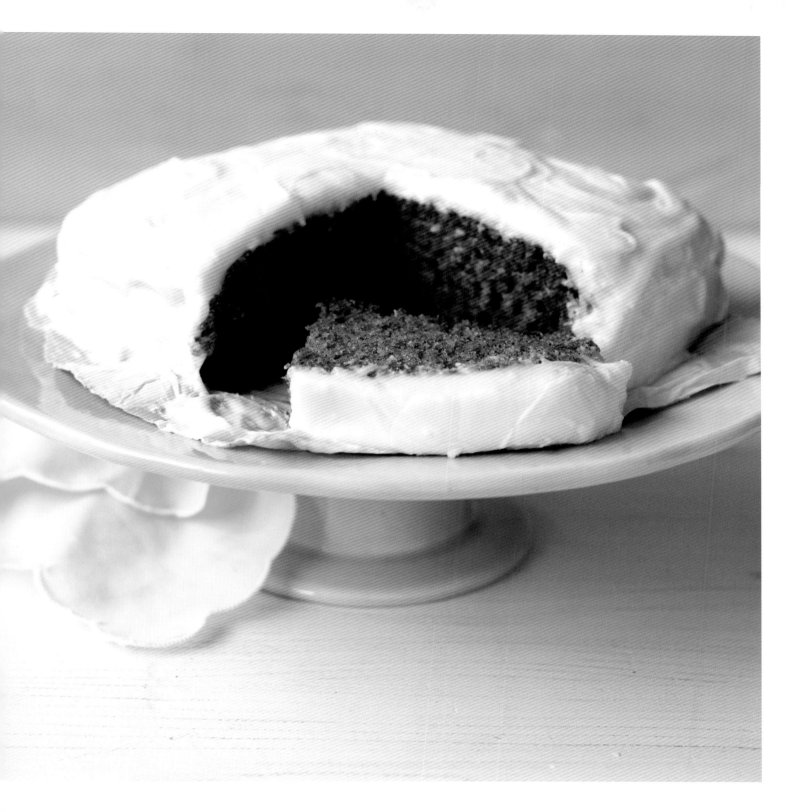

MARSHMALLOW CANELÉ

Canelés are an extraordinary cake native to Bordeaux. A rum and vanilla custard is baked at high temperature in a fluted mold to give a dense custardy center surrounded by a caramelized sugar crust. Here, vanilla marshmallow is baked and served with a rum and chocolate sauce.

INGREDIENTS

½ quantity ingredients for vanilla
   marshmallow mix (see page 10)
3 ½ ounces (100g) semisweet chocolate
½ tablespoon cornstarch
1 cup (240ml) milk
1 piece of orange rind
Seeds from 1 vanilla bean
2 tablespoons dark rum

METHOD

Grease 8 canelé molds. It's a careful business getting the marshmallow to fill them completely and make sure they release easily.

Make the vanilla marshmallow mix following the method on page 10. Fill a pastry bag with the mix and pipe it carefully and meticulously into the canelé molds. You'll find this easier if you use a small ¼–⅜-inch (0.5–1cm) plain round tip. Fill to the top, then level off with a spatula. Let the marshmallow set. Gently push the marshmallows out. If they are difficult to remove, then submerging the bottom of the silicone in hot water for a few seconds will help to release them.

Turn the canelés upright and place in small individual earthenware dishes. Blowtorch the sides of the canelé until blistered and golden. You want the marshmallows to retain their shape but to be as molten and warm as possible at their core.

To make the sauce, blend the chocolate in a food processor or finely chop it. Stir together the cornstarch and chocolate. Place in a saucepan with the milk over low heat and stir continuously. As the chocolate starts to melt, add the orange rind and vanilla seeds. Keep stirring until the sauce is glossy, thick, and smooth. Stir in the rum. Drizzle over the canelés.

Serves 8

TIP

Canelé molds are available online or in specialty cookware stores. You need silicone molds—not the metal ones.

HOT CHOCOLATE MARSHMALLOW FONDANTS

Developing this recipe was a nightmare journey of warm chocolate and molten marshmallow.
You'll thank me for my selfless determination. The already molten chocolate core melts the
marshmallow into a fabulous chocolate marshmallow ooze fest.

INGREDIENTS

3 ½ tablespoons (50g) butter
Unsweetened cocoa for dusting
3 ½ ounces (100g) semisweet chocolate
7 tablespoons (100g) butter
½ cup (100g) superfine sugar
2 eggs
2 egg yolks
¾ cup (100g) all-purpose flour
Pinch of salt
4 large round marshmallows of your choice

4 dariole molds

METHOD

Preheat the oven to 400°F (200°C). Melt the 3 ½ tablespoons butter and brush the insides of the dariole molds with it. Sift the cocoa into the greased molds, ensuring there's an even covering. Tap the molds upside down to remove excess.

Melt the chocolate and butter together in a heatproof bowl over a saucepan of barely simmering water (bain-marie or double-boiler).

Place the sugar, eggs, and egg yolks in the bowl of a free-standing mixer or use a bowl and electric handmixer. Whisk until the mixture is pale and voluminous. Sift in the flour and salt and fold to combine. Fold in the melted chocolate and butter.

Spoon the mix into the molds to half full. Press a marshmallow into the center of the batter. Top up the molds so that they are two-thirds full.

Bake in the oven for exactly 10 minutes. The fondant should be firm (other than the melted marshmallow poking through) on the top but still loose in the center.

During baking, the marshmallow will puff up and peak through the top of the chocolate mix. Place a small plate on top of the fondant to squash it back down. Flip the mold and plate over and tap. If the molds were evenly and well lined, the fondant will be released.

Eat with custard, cream, or fresh berries.

Serves 4

COLD CHOCOLATE MARSHMALLOW FONDANTS

Slightly easier to construct, this chocolate fondant can be made well ahead of time but still has that soft marshmallow core—wow.

INGREDIENTS

For the marshmallow:
2 egg whites (2 ½ ounces/70g)
⅔ cup (120g) superfine sugar
Seeds from 1 vanilla bean

10 ounces (300g) semisweet
  chocolate
3 ½ tablespoons (50g) butter
3 eggs
¾ cup (150g) superfine sugar
1 ¼ cups (300ml) heavy cream

4 dariole molds

METHOD

First make the marshmallow core. Combine the egg whites and superfine sugar in a heatproof bowl over a saucepan of simmering water (bain-marie or double-boiler) and whisk continuously until the sugar has dissolved and the mixture has reached 143°F (61°C) on a digital candy thermometer. Remove from the heat and whisk to stiff peaks in a free-standing mixer or with an electric handmixer. Add the vanilla seeds.

Spoon or scrape this mix into a pastry bag with a plain round tip about ½ inch (1.25cm) in diameter. Set to one side.

Melt the chocolate and butter in a bain-marie or double-boiler. Remove from the heat and let cool slightly.

Place the eggs in the bowl of a free-standing mixer or use a regular bowl and electric handmixer. Whisk the eggs for 30 seconds. Heat the superfine sugar and 6 tablespoons (100ml) water in a small saucepan to make a sugar syrup. Heat to 237°F (114°C) then pour in a thin stream onto the eggs while you whisk. This creates a pâte à bombe. Whisk until pale and thick and tripled in volume. Fold the melted chocolate mixture into the pâte à bombe.

Whip the heavy cream to soft peaks, and fold into the chocolate and egg mixture. Spoon this mixture into four dariole molds or ramekins until half full. Pipe the fresh marshmallow mix into the center of the fondant. Fill the mold to the top with more chocolate mix and smooth flat. Let set in the refrigerator for at least 4 hours.

To remove from the molds, place a hot cloth around the edges of the molds or dunk them carefully in a bowl of hot water. If they are difficult, the edges may be loosened with a knife. Tip them out and enjoy.

Serves 4

MARSHMALLOW BAKED APPLES

The dessert universe is filled with many greats—but twinkling away at the outer rim is the baked apple. Always there, waiting for you. When the rain is a-pourin' and the wind is a-blowin' it soothes and comforts, and well . . . everything will be all right.

INGREDIENTS

4 cooking apples
1 handful of your favorite marshmallows, cut into ½-inch (1.25cm) cubes but reserving 4 for decoration
¼ cup (60g) light brown sugar
½ teaspoon ground cinnamon
¼ teaspoon ground ginger
½ cup (100g) golden raisins
3 ½ tablespoons (50g) butter

METHOD

Preheat the oven to 350°F (180°C).

Core the apples and cut through the skin around the equator of the apple. Place the apples in a baking dish.

Mix together all the ingredients other than the butter.

Pack as much of this mix as possible into the center of the apples. Cut the butter into four pieces and rest a piece on top of each apple.

Cook them in the oven for 30–40 minutes. How long they need will depend on the size of the apple. They are done when a fork passes easily into the soft fluffy flesh. The marshmallow in the core of the apple will melt, so add a reserved marshmallow on the top of the apple to heighten the presentation.

Eat with lovely ice cream or ladles of custard.

Serves 4

LEMON MARSHMALLOW MERINGUE PIE

Using marshmallow instead of meringue adds a great texture to this classic. It holds its shape and crisps up wonderfully. Packing the marshmallows closely creates an impressive crust.

INGREDIENTS

For the pastry:
7 tablespoons (100g) butter, softened
½ cup (65g) confectioners' sugar
1 vanilla bean
2 ½ tablespoons (20g) almond meal
1 egg (1 ½ ounces/40g)
1 ⅓ cups (170g) all-purpose flour
Or store-bought good-quality all-butter short crust pastry would be fine here

Juice and zest of 4 lemons
2 tablespoons cornstarch
½ cup (100g) superfine sugar
6 tablespoons (80g) butter
1 egg
4 egg yolks
½ quantity vanilla marshmallows (see page 10), cut into different-size cubes

METHOD

Mix the butter and confectioners' sugar in the bowl of a free-standing mixer until well combined, pale in color, and beginning to become fluffy. If using a handheld electric mixer, scrape the sides of the bowl and mix again.

Split the vanilla bean, scrape out the seeds, and add to the butter and sugar. Scrape the sides of the bowl down again and add the almond meal.

Beat the egg and slowly add to the mixture bit by bit. It's crucial at this stage to ensure you keep scraping down the sides of the bowl to keep all the ingredients well combined. Add the flour in one go and mix in. Bring together as a ball, cover with plastic wrap, and chill.

Preheat the oven to 325°F (160°C). Grease and flour a 9-inch (22.5cm) round tart pan. Roll out the pastry on a floured surface to about ⅛ inch (3mm) thickness. Line the tart pan with the pastry, then line the pastry with baking parchment and fill with pie weights. Bake blind until the bottom of the pastry shell is an even light brown. Remove the baking parchment and pie weights.

Place the lemon juice and zest in a small saucepan and bring to a simmer. Turn off the heat and let the zest infuse the juice for 15 minutes or so. Then strain the zest through a fine strainer. Mix together cornstarch and infused lemon juice and add to the sugar. Add ⅞ cup (200ml) of water and heat until thick and smooth. Remove from the heat and whisk in the butter. Whisk the whole egg and yolks to combine, then add that to the lemon mix. Return to the heat for a couple of minutes and stir continuously until thick and it bubbles like a volcanic mud pool. Cool.

Preheat the oven to 350°F (180°C). Pour the lemon mix into the baked pastry shell. Arrange the cubes of marshmallow all over the top of the lemon filling. Bake in the oven for 5–10 minutes until the marshmallow is toasted all over.

MARSHMALLOW PUMPKIN PIE

Following the same principle as the lemon marshmallow meringue pie (see page 127) the filling is a deeply spiced pumpkin layer. Take one slice as required after building bonfires and sweeping up fall leaves.

INGREDIENTS

1 quantity ingredients for pastry
    (see page 127)
1 ¼ pounds (600g) pumpkin or
    butternut squash, peeled and
    cut into 1-inch (2.5cm) cubes
⅔ cup (120g) unrefined superfine sugar
½ teaspoon salt
Pinch of grated nutmeg
½ teaspoon ground cinnamon
¼ teaspoon ground cloves
1 egg
2 egg yolks
⅔ cup (160ml) milk
2 tablespoons (30g) butter, melted
½ quantity vanilla marshmallows
    (see page 10), cut into
    different-size cubes
Confectioners' sugar and ground
    cinnamon, for dusting (optional)

METHOD

Make the pastry shell following the recipe on page 127 and bake it blind (lined with baking parchment and filled with ceramic baking beans or dried pulses). Steam the pumpkin until a fork easily passes into the flesh. Let cool, then mash and pass through a strainer. Preheat oven to 350°F (180°C).

Combine the sugar with the salt and spices. Add the egg, egg yolks, milk, and butter. Stir in the pumpkin and pour into the tart shell. Bake for 15–20 minutes until the edges are starting to set but the center is still a little loose. Cover the surface with marshmallows and return to the oven for 5–10 minutes until golden and crisp.

Let cool, then dust with confectioners' sugar mixed with a little more ground cinnamon, if using.

Chapter 9

HOLIDAYS

Snow-white marshmallows are perfect for celebrating winter holidays—
who can resist a marshmallow snowman? But don't save them for the
colder months. A Valentine's Day, Easter, or Halloween party will all
benefit from a heart-, egg-, or pumpkin-shaped marshmallow or two.

VALENTINE'S MARSHMALLOWS

Perhaps you'll lose out on the day because "they aren't real roses, are they" but think of what you'll gain in "ah, cute, he/she made me marshmallows." We've previously established that marshmallows are the key to personal happiness—that extends to all aspects of your love life.

METHOD

Using the rose marshmallow recipe on page 36, make a sheet of suitable pink and fragrant marshmallow.

Contrast these with a second tray of white vanilla marshmallows (see page 10). Cut out small and medium heart shapes, and dust.

These could be given in beautiful ribbon bags or turned into a bunch of roses by securing them on skewers or thick sugarcraft wire.

MARSHMALLOW EASTER EGGS

Marshmallow is easily molded using Easter egg-shaped molds. Meticulously grease the molds, then dust with the 50/50 confectioners' sugar and cornstarch mix (see page 10).

METHOD

Make your favorite marshmallows. A few drops of pastel shade food coloring would heighten the Easter appeal. Spoon the marshmallow into the mold and smooth it flat to the top of the mold. Let set.

To join the two halves of the egg gently, warm the exposed surface of each marshmallow half. Push together and let them set. Carefully coax out of the mold, warming them slightly if the marshmallow is difficult to remove.

Cover the join with suitable springtime ribbon. Keep them simple and perfect.

HOT CROSS BUN MARSHMALLOWS

Here, the classic hot cross bun flavors are mixed with fluffy marshmallow. The subtle spicing and fruit work together well with the sweet marshmallow. As with real hot cross buns, they are far too tasty to make only once a year.

INGREDIENTS

1 quantity ingredients for vanilla
  marshmallow mix (see page 10)
½ cup (75g) golden raisins
⅓ cup (50g) chopped candied peel
Zest of 1 orange
1 apple, peeled, cored, and finely chopped
1 teaspoon ground cinnamon
Natural brown food coloring

METHOD

Make the marshmallow mix following the method on page 10. After the final whisking stage, remove 3 tablespoons of the plain mix and set aside. Add the golden raisins, candied peel, orange zest, apple, and ground cinnamon to the remaining marshmallow mix and stir well to combine. Add a few drops of brown coloring.

Lightly grease a cookie sheet with vegetable oil. Scrape the marshmallow mix into a pastry bag with a wide ¾-inch (2cm) tip, and pipe small 2-inch (5cm) rounds onto the cookie sheet. Alternatively, shape with spoons dipped in warm water. You should have approximately 20 circles of marshmallow.

Gently heat the reserved 3 tablespoons marshmallow to melt. When runny, either drizzle or pipe small white crosses over the top of each marshmallow bun.

Makes 20 marshmallows

PUMPKIN SPICED MARSHMALLOWS

Inspired by your favorite Halloween latte flavoring, don't make these unless you're going to cut the marshmallows into circles and decorate as pumpkins. It would be mean spirited not to. You could add a few tablespoons of puréed pumpkin or squash to these marshmallows, but really these are all about the spicing and do not need it.

INGREDIENTS

1 quantity ingredients for vanilla marshmallow mix
    (see page 10)
Natural orange food coloring
½ tablespoon ground cinnamon
½ teaspoon grated nutmeg
½ teaspoon ground ginger
¼ teaspoon ground allspice

Black edible pen or, if your piping skills are up to it,
    water icing colored black

METHOD

Make the marshmallow mix following the method on page 10, and whisk in the coloring and spices during the final whisking stage. Scrape the mix into an oiled baking pan and let set. Once set, cut out with a round or pumpkin cutter. Draw on eyes and big teeth with black pen or water icing. Eat or give away to trick or treaters.

CANDY CANE MARSHMALLOW TWISTS

Save this recipe for around December 21. Put on some Christmas carols and a cozy sweater and proceed. These can be flavored with peppermint extract or melted candy canes. As much as the marshmallow is tasty, the real enjoyment here is in the piping and the twisting.

INGREDIENTS

1 quantity ingredients for vanilla
    marshmallow mix (see page 10)
3 ½ ounces (100g) candy canes, or
    peppermint extract
Natural red food coloring
1 quantity 50/50 coating (see page 10)

METHOD

Make the marshmallow mix following the method on page 10. While the marshmallow is having its final whisk, and if you're using them, melt the candy canes in a small saucepan. In all honesty, peppermint flavoring will do the job of making these marshmallows taste like candy canes. However, the idea of a recipe that has candy canes as an ingredient is irresistible. They take a while to melt, and you need to keep stirring constantly, but they will and it's very satisfying.

Tip the melted candy canes into the whisking marshmallow mix or add in a few drops of peppermint extract. Divide the mix in two and add red food coloring to one half to give a deep pink color.

Fit a disposable pastry bag (see Resources, page 144) with a plain round 2 ¾–4-inch (7cm–10cm) tip. Grease a cookie sheet. Pipe long strips of one color and then long strips of the other color. Let the marshmallows dry slightly, enough to handle them. Lay a white strip next to a pink. Press down one end of the marshmallow strip so it's fixed. Take the other end and slowly twist the strips together. Repeat until all the strips are used.

Dust with the 50/50 coating mix and let set overnight. Cut into lengths and use to decorate trees, fill stockings, and to leave out for Santa to treat Rudolph.

CHRISTMAS MARSHMALLOWS

Now is the time to dig out the Christmas cookie cutters, edible glitters, colored icings, and ribbon. Prepare these as perfect candies to produce at a moment's notice for unexpected guests or packaged beautifully as stocking fillers. It's easy enough to make a small hole in a marshmallow and hang with ribbon from a Christmas tree. They will keep okay like that for 24 hours or so and then become rather dry and hard.

INGREDIENTS

1 quantity ingredients for vanilla
  marshmallow mix (see page 10)
Zest of 2 oranges
¾ cup (100g) dried cranberries

CRANBERRY & ORANGE

Make the marshmallow mix following the method on page 10. Add the orange zest and cranberries after the final whisking stage. Scrape into a lightly oiled baking pan. Let set, then cut into shapes.

INGREDIENTS

1 quantity ingredients for vanilla
  marshmallow mix (see page 10)
About ¼ cup (60ml) gingerbread syrup
  (available from coffee and tea suppliers—
  usually used to flavor your favorite latte)
1 teaspoon ground ginger
1 quantity 50/50 coating (see page 10)

GINGERBREAD

Make the marshmallow mix following the method on page 10. Add the gingerbread syrup at the final whisking stage. Add more, or less, to your taste. Scrape the mix into a lightly oiled baking pan and let set. Add the ground ginger to the 50/50 coating mix. Once set, cut into shapes and dust with the ginger coating mix.

CHRISTMAS PUDDING MARSHMALLOWS

These dark-chocolate puddings hide a sweet surprise—a mouthful of sweet marshmallow rather than the traditional dried fruits. White chocolate and candy holly complete the festive look.

METHOD

Pipe vanilla marshmallow mix (see page 10) into demisphere molds, or pipe freehand pudding shapes onto an oiled cookie sheet. Let set.

Melt semisweet chocolate in a heatproof bowl over a saucepan of barely simmering water (bain-marie or double-boiler). Remove the marshmallows from the mold and push a toothpick into each base. Dip them into the chocolate. Skewer the chocolate-covered marshmallows into a piece of Styrofoam and let dry. Once set, drizzle white chocolate melted in the same way or thick water icing over the marshmallows to represent the custard.

Finish decorating with sugar paste holly and berries bought from a specialty cake decorating store or made at home.

MARSHMALLOW SNOWMEN

A batch of vanilla marshmallow mix (see page 10) is quickly transformed into these festive delights.

METHOD

Whisk the marshmallow mixture well. Fit a disposable pastry bag (see Resources, page 144) with a plain ½-inch (1.25cm) tip. Lightly grease a cookie sheet with oil and pipe a large round base. Holding the tip approximately ¾ inch (2cm) above the surface will help create a nice round body. Pipe all the bases.

Separately, pipe medium-size balls for the bodies and small balls for the heads. Dust your hands with confectioner's sugar and roll each ball a little to round them out. To assemble, carefully slice the top off each base and press bases, bodies, and heads together. Let set, then dust lightly with 50/50 coating before decorating as this will make the snowmen easier to handle.

Depending on your piping skills, you may find you are making small spikes on the marshmallow when you finish piping. These may be flattened as you go by wetting your finger or a clean paintbrush with warm water and smoothing the marshmallow flat.

Features may be drawn on with edible pens or piped with chocolate or water icing. Chocolates, candies, and other confectionery can be utilized as arms, hats, and scarves.

Even simpler versions can be constructed using circular-cut marshmallows skewered on lollipop sticks.

MARSHMALLOW BÛCHE DE NOEL

Yule log pans are easy to track down online. They are a great mold to have up your sleeve. Anything shaped in it is immediately festive and exciting. Use it for chocolate mousses, sponge cakes, and even savory pâtés and terrines. This recipe is a mix of marshmallow and nougat. Fluffy marshmallow punctuated with fruity, nutty, and chocolaty nuggets—all bound together in a richly spiced marshmallow. Feel free to change the fruit and nut additions to your preference.

INGREDIENTS

1 quantity 50/50 coating (see page 10)
1 ½ quantities ingredients for vanilla
   marshmallow mix (see page 10)
½ teaspoon ground cinnamon
Finely grated zest of 1 mandarin or satsuma
Finely grated zest of ½ lemon
3 tablespoons candied peel
3 tablespoons candied cherries, halved
¼ cup (1 ounce/25g) golden raisins
3 tablespoons whole unsalted pistachios
3 ounces (75g) semisweet chocolate,
   coarsely chopped

Lightly grease a 10-inch (25.5cm) yule log pan with oil and dust with some of the 50/50 coating mix. Be meticulous with this as otherwise you'll have all sorts of bother removing it from the pan after it has set.

Make the marshmallow mix following the method on page 10. During the final whisk, add the cinnamon, candied peel, and fruit zest. After that's incorporated, add the fruit and nuts. Just before scraping out into the bûche mold, add the coarsely chopped chocolate.

Scrape out into the bûche mold and let set. Remove carefully from the pan. You may need to warm the outside of the pan with a hot cloth or dunk the underside in hot water for a few seconds if it proves tricky to remove.

Present on a platter, domed side up, and dust with more of the 50/50 coating. Decorate the marshmallow with extra candied fruit and nuts along the top. Cut slices for deserving guests.

INDEX

RESOURCES

SPICES AND CITRIC ACID
The Spice House www.thespicehouse.com
My Spice Sage www.myspicesage.com
The Savory Spice Shop www.savoryspiceshop.com
Kalustyans www.kalustyans.com
Penzeys www.penzeys.com
The Chef Shop www.chefshop.com
Dean and Deluca www.deananddeluca.com
Gourmet Food Store www.gourmetfoodstore.com
Williams-Sonoma www.williams-sonoma.com

FLAVORINGS
Gourmet Food Store www.gourmetfoodstore.com
Marque Foods www.marquefoods.com
Sur la Table www.surlatable.com

BAKING EQUIPMENT AND INGREDIENTS
N.Y. Cake www.nycake.com
Pastry Items www.pastryitems.com
Kitchen Krafts www.kitchenkrafts.com
Sasa Demarle www.demarleusa.com

FRUIT POWDERS AND FREEZE-DRIED FRUIT
The Great American Spice Co. www.americanspice.com
Crunchies http://crunchiesfood.com
North Bay Trading Co. www.northbaytrading.com

FOOD-GRADE ACETATE AND FLAVORINGS
Kerekes www.bakedeco.com
Pastry Chef Central www.pastrychef.com

LEAF GELATIN
Modernist Pantry www.modernistpantry.com
Pastry Chef Central www.pastrychef.com
Kitchen Krafts www.kitchenkrafts.com
Gourmet Food Store www.gourmetfoodstore.com

CARRAGEENAN
Modernist Pantry www.modernistpantry.com

GLUCOSE SYRUP
Kitchen Krafts www.kitchenkrafts.com

KITCHEN EQUIPMENT
Kitchen Aid www.kitchenaid.com
Magimix www.magimix.com
Kenwood www.kenwood.com
Microplane www.microplane.com

ACKNOWLEDGMENTS

I'd like to thank the team at Macarons & More and our customers for their support.